Praise for *Whe*

"At once thoughtful and uplifting, insight into the challenges our re transition back into a society. Th ....se, Tom's challenges are not atypical among those seeking to heal the moral injuries of war. By recounting his healing journey, Tom paints a vivid and hopeful picture of what is possible for those burdened by the scars of war and provides a road map to that healing place."

— **Mike Haynie, PhD,** Vice Chancellor for Strategic Initiatives and Innovation, Barnes Professor of Entrepreneurship, and executive director of the Institute for Veterans and Military Families (IVMF), Syracuse University

"A captivating personal journey that forces you to rethink the derivative impacts of military service. Tom Voss writes with compelling immediacy about the importance of community and a holistic approach to the reintegration of veterans into the fabric of our society."

— **Brian E. Kinsella,** cofounder and chairman of Stop Soldier Suicide

"The gripping tale of Tom Voss's fight, in and out of the warzone, and his incredible journey, across the country and around the world, will inspire countless others, leaving them with a sense of purpose and hope."

— **David Shulkin, MD,** ninth secretary of the US Department of Veterans Affairs and author of *It Shouldn't Be This Hard to Serve Your Country*

"For nearly the last twenty years, our country has been at war. In that time, there have been many books published by veterans detailing their experiences. In most cases, however, the discerning reader can sense an editing of the story by the author as it is retold. Not in this case. Tom Voss attacks the truth in his story with a furious intensity, and there's an inherent beauty that it creates. I simply couldn't stop reading it. Moral injury may be a hallmark injury of the global war on terror, and Tom is one of the most important spokesmen of our generation. His message of personal responsibility in the healing process is not only timely but timeless. I'm confident this book will resonate with everyone in some unique way."

— **John Pinter,** executive director of
Team Red, White & Blue

"Like traditional warrior societies, the United States has an effective system for creating warriors out of raw recruits. Unlike traditional warrior societies, it lacks an effective cultural system for welcoming warriors returning to civilian life and providing resources for the return journey of reflection, healing, and spiritual recovery from the psychological and spiritual wounds of war. Having discovered for themselves that drugs, alcohol, and conversations with medical professionals are inadequate substitutes for a true warrior reintegration tradition, Tom Voss and his fellow veteran Anthony create a process for themselves and other warriors in their walk across the country, a physical and spiritual journey of 2,700 miles that gives Tom the time and space to make peace with the ghosts of the dead and find a new path among the living. Well written, engaging, and thought provoking, *Where War Ends* is recommended for anyone who cares about veterans and would like to better understand their journey back from war."

— **Holly Arrow,** professor of psychology at the
Groups & War Lab, University of Oregon

WHERE
WAR
ENDS

RECOVERING FROM PTSD AND
MORAL INJURY THROUGH MEDITATION

WHERE WAR ENDS

A COMBAT VETERAN'S
2,700-MILE JOURNEY TO HEAL

TOM VOSS AND REBECCA ANNE NGUYEN

New World Library
Novato, California

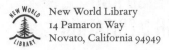

New World Library
14 Pamaron Way
Novato, California 94949

Copyright © 2019 by Tom Voss and Rebecca Anne Nguyen

All rights reserved. This book may not be reproduced in whole or in part, stored in a retrieval system, or transmitted in any form or by any means — electronic, mechanical, or other — without written permission from the publisher, except by a reviewer, who may quote brief passages in a review.

The material in this book is intended for education. It is not meant to take the place of diagnosis and treatment by a qualified medical practitioner or therapist. No expressed or implied guarantee of the effects of the use of the recommendations can be given or liability taken.

Text design by Tona Pearce Myers

Library of Congress Cataloging-in-Publication Data
Names: Voss, Tom (Thomas P.), author. | Nguyen, Rebecca Anne, date, author.
Title: Where war ends : a combat veteran's 2,700-mile journey to heal : recovering
    from PTSD and moral injury through meditation / Tom Voss and Rebecca Anne
    Nguyen.
Description: Novato, California : New World Library, [2019] | Includes bibliograph-
    ical references. | Summary: "A veteran of the Iraq War describes his struggle to
    heal from Post Traumatic Stress Disorder and come to terms with the horrors of
    combat"-- Provided by publisher.
Identifiers: LCCN 2019022222 (print) | LCCN 2019981387 (ebook) | ISBN
    9781608685998 | ISBN 9781608686001 (ebook)
Subjects: LCSH: Voss, Tom (Thomas P.) | Post-traumatic stress disorder--Patients--
    United States--Biography. | Veterans--United States--Biography. | Post-traumatic
    stress disorder--Treatment. | Veterans--Mental health--United States. | Medita-
    tion--Therapeutic use. | Disabled veterans--Rehabilitation--United States. | Iraq
    War, 2003-2011--Moral and ethical aspects.
Classification: LCC RC552.P67 V67 2019 (print) | LCC RC552.P67 (ebook) | DDC
    616.85/210092 [B]--dc23
LC record available at https://lccn.loc.gov/2019022222
LC ebook record available at https://lccn.loc.gov/2019981387
First printing, October 2019
ISBN 978-1-60868-599-8
Ebook ISBN 978-1-60868-600-1

Printed in Canada on 100% postconsumer-waste recycled paper

 New World Library is proud to be a Gold Certified Environmentally
Responsible Publisher. Publisher certification awarded by Green Press
Initiative.

10   9   8   7   6   5   4   3   2   1

For Mack, Solo, and the Assassins of the 3-21 Infantry
— T.V.

For Tom
— R.A.N.

The wound is the place where the light enters you.

— Rūmī

Most names in this book have been changed to protect the privacy of those who survived and the memory of those who did not.

CONTENTS

Part 2: Mobile

Part 3: Still

PREFACE

Moral injury is a wound to the soul. It happens when you participate in or witness things that transgress your deepest beliefs about right and wrong. It is extreme trauma that manifests as grief, sorrow, shame, guilt, or any combination of those things. It shows up as negative thoughts, self-hatred, hatred of others, feelings of regret, obsessive behaviors, destructive tendencies, suicidal ideation, and all-consuming isolation.

You may experience moral injury if you've survived abuse, witnessed violence, participated in the chaos of combat, or experienced any form of trauma that's changed your understanding of what you, or other human beings, are morally capable of. For many combat veterans, moral injury is inflicted during war, when they are split into two different versions of themselves: the person they were *before* war, whose morality was ingrained in them by their parents, religion, culture, and society, and the person they became *during* war, whose morality was replaced with a sense of right and wrong that helped them survive in a war zone.

When the smoke clears and the chaos of war ends, these two selves, with two different sets of moral values, confront each other and continue to battle. The prewar self points to the postwar self and says, "Hey! I know what you did. I know what you saw. You were wrong, you are bad, and you can never be good again."

A soldier may experience moral injury when reflecting on his or her actions during combat. But they can also experience moral injury by bearing witness to the actions of others. The cool indifference of a commanding officer as he stands over a dying civilian; the capture and torture of men who are known to be innocent; the bomb that was planted purposefully to destroy human life: all can call into question our deeply held cultural belief that all people, deep down, are innately good. Bearing witness to the moral indifference of others, or the premeditation of violence, is enough to warp your understanding of morality and make you question the moral character of everyone you meet. This makes it hard for veterans to trust other people and to assume the best in others, and in themselves.

In addition to participating in and witnessing violence, there's a third, lesser-known cause of moral injury that impacts soldiers returning from war. It's the sense of confusion, powerlessness, and betrayal that soldiers feel when they come home and try to transition back to civilian life.

Some people call them heroes, but most veterans don't feel like heroes, so there's a disconnect between the actual experience of war and the perceived experience of it. That disconnect makes veterans feel isolated and misunderstood. Others question veterans' moral character for participating in wars started on false pretenses, or in any war at all. A small but vocal minority calls veterans leeches or lazy. They say veterans are taking advantage of the government, and subsequently taxpayers, when they partake in the benefits promised to them for their service. When faced with these accusations, misunderstandings, and questions, veterans start to question themselves.

Moral injury is emotional, psychological, and spiritual. This makes it different from post-traumatic stress disorder, which is more of a physiological reaction — the brain and body's responses to extreme, prolonged stress or fear. Some of the symptoms of PTSD — nightmares, flashbacks, insomnia, disassociation — can be stabilized with medication. But moral injury doesn't seem to respond to medication, at least not permanently. Not at the soul level.

Time in and of itself is also not enough to heal the suffering of moral injury. Time can soften the sting of moral injury, but it can also harden memories, making emotional scar tissue even tougher to heal. That's what happens if you leave a wound to fester without tending to it. And that's why so many Vietnam veterans take psychiatric medications for decades and then, when they retire or divorce, or are otherwise forced to face themselves and their past, still find a world of pain waiting for them. The medication has only treated their symptoms, not the root cause of those symptoms. The wound can grow so big, so consuming, it feels like the only way to escape it is death.

The VA estimates that in the United States, twenty veterans take their lives every day.* While the majority of those who die by suicide are over the age of fifty, the number of younger vets who contribute to that twenty-a-day statistic is steadily

---

* Office of Public and Intergovernmental Affairs, "VA Releases National Suicide Data Report," US Department of Veterans Affairs, June 18, 2018, https://www.va.gov/opa/pressrel/pressrelease.cfm?id=4074.

increasing. If the veterans of the wars in Iraq and Afghanistan fail to acknowledge and heal moral injury, the millennial generation of veterans will continue to face the same fate as those who've gone before.

This book offers an unexpected antidote to moral injury. It shows how healing is possible even when traditional methods like talk therapy, EMDR (Eye Movement Desensitization and Reprocessing), and medication have failed. It reveals a healing method that is accessible to anyone who's willing to sit still for a few moments and just breathe. It shows how, as soon as an individual is willing to take responsibility for his or her own healing, grace rushes in to relieve the pain, unravel traumatic memories, and release the past for good. It shows how meditation, breath work, and the body's natural intelligence can help heal deep trauma in ways the mind can't. You can't *think* yourself into feeling better. You can't *will* yourself to heal. But in taking on a discipline like meditation, you create the space where healing can happen, naturally. This book shows how the act and discipline of meditation can redeem a life — no matter how deep the wound.

The responsibility to acknowledge, accept, and heal from moral injury doesn't just belong to those suffering from moral injury. When we send our youth into battle on our behalf, we are complicit in their actions. We are responsible for bearing our portion of the pain those actions cause. And in taking responsibility, we are empowered to help these women and men rebuild their moral scaffolding, reclaim their place in the society they volunteered to protect, and remember what it means to be human — and to belong.

— Tom Voss and Rebecca Anne Nguyen

INTRODUCTION

From 2003 to 2006, I served on active duty in the US Army. In October 2004 I was deployed to Mosul, Iraq, to support Operation Iraqi Freedom. I served as an infantry scout in the battalion scout-sniper platoon in the 3rd Battalion, 21st Infantry Regiment, an element of the 1st Brigade 25th Infantry Division — one of the army's first Stryker infantry brigades. During the twelve months I spent in Iraq, I participated in hundreds of combat missions, convoys, security patrols, raids, area-clearance operations, and humanitarian-relief operations. In 2006 I separated from the army with an honorable discharge.

And then I came home.

This book is about what happened next. It's about the feelings I carried inside that no one, including me, talked about: feelings of grief, shame, guilt, and sorrow about the things I'd seen and done in Iraq. Those feelings didn't change or go away, no matter what I tried. And I tried everything: talk therapy,

EMDR, peer-support groups, alcohol, legal drugs, illegal drugs, you name it.

I decided to walk across the country because I had no other choice. I knew that if I didn't take an extreme step to heal from trauma, the trauma I had experienced in Iraq would consume me and I would end my own life.

Walking across the country gave me the time and space I needed to heal. Walking was a way to convene with nature, which had always been a healing, uplifting force in my life. Some of my happiest childhood memories are of taking long walks in the forests and trails of northern Wisconsin. My dad taught my sister and me to respect the natural world and to view it with wonder. The wind in the trees, the deer hiding in the brush, the ripples on the surface of a still pond: all had something to teach us, if only we'd get quiet and listen. So I decided to walk from Milwaukee to Los Angeles to get back to that place — a place where the movement of my body on the outside made me still enough on the inside to learn the lessons nature had to teach me.

On that walk, nature became my healer and my teacher again. And like any good teacher, nature led me to other teachers — Native American healers, meditation instructors, and spiritual devotees. Nature even threw in a controversial Trappist monk and a world-renowned Indian guru for good measure.

It was about a month after I finished my 2,700-mile journey across America that I first learned about something called moral injury. This was the answer I'd been looking for — the cause of the symptoms I'd been battling for so long. Moral injury was the root of all the grief, shame, sorrow, and guilt I'd been feeling. It was a wound to the soul that had destroyed my sense of morality, demolished my moral architecture, and confused my moral place in society. Once I knew what had been causing those deep, emotional symptoms — what was *beneath* the depression and *behind* the anxiety — the healing process could truly begin.

During the five months I spent walking across the country, and in the years that followed, I've learned healing methods that I believe can help people who suffer from moral injury and extreme trauma. Meditation, yoga, and breath work have offered relief and healing I never could have imagined, both for me and for the other veterans I've worked with. I truly believe that if you're willing to put in the time, these methods will work for you, too.

The end of my walk across America was just the beginning of a healing journey that I'm still on, and that I'll continue on for the rest of my life. I hope that reading my story or watching my story in the documentary film *Almost Sunrise* will help you on your own journey to heal from moral injury. At the very least, I hope your sense of hope will be renewed by learning about someone who knows what it is to give up on life, and himself, completely.

It only takes a single flicker of light to cut through the darkness. And it only takes a single glimmer of hope to start healing from moral injury.

It's my dream that this book will help you hang on to that sense of hope, no matter how small, with all your might.

You are not alone.

Healing is possible.

I'm living proof of that.

— Tom Voss
Ojai, California
October 2019

Part 1

STUCK

Out of suffering have emerged the strongest souls;
the most massive characters are seared with scars.

— Khalil Gibran

1
TIME TO GO

On a warm, gray morning, as I lay in bed in my apartment, someone knocked at the door.

"I should get up and answer it," I thought.

The thought hovered above me in the air before disintegrating to nothing.

Knock, knock, knock.

The pounding in my head thumped out of time with the pounding on the door, like a drummer who couldn't catch the beat.

It couldn't be Kimmy. The last time I'd seen her, I'd gone to visit her at work. A handsome, stone-faced marine glared at me from his barstool while Kimmy rearranged bottles of rail liquor behind the bar. She'd smiled at me, but that guy's unblinking stare spoke for both of them — I'd been replaced. I took a step back, turned, and retreated out of her life.

Get up.

Get up and open the door.

It couldn't be my mom. She was at work, teaching at a private school in the River Hills neighborhood of Milwaukee. My dad had retired from social work, but he kept a strict schedule that demanded his time and attention at particular hours of the day: breakfast from 8:00 to 8:30 AM, exercise till 9:15, guitar practice, gardening, lunch, and a postlunch nap that didn't count as a nap because he took it sitting up in his favorite chair. Dad wouldn't miss guitar practice to drive across town to my East Side apartment unannounced.

The weight of the furniture in the room seemed to press into me until it felt like my body was sinking through the bed. I imagined myself lying on the floor, pinned underneath the cracked feet of the hand-me-down dresser. The embroidered peacocks on the bright-green couch beneath the window stared at me with judging eyes. *Get up, you worthless piece of shit.*

Knock, knock, knock, knock, knock.

Was my sister in town? I couldn't keep track anymore. Since graduating high school early, she'd moved from Milwaukee to Syracuse, then back to Milwaukee, then to Miami, then back to Milwaukee, then to Madison, then back to Milwaukee, then to Los Angeles, then back to Milwaukee, then back to Los Angeles, then to Taiwan, then to Evanston, Illinois, and then — you guessed it — back to Milwaukee again. She'd moved away and moved back to this town like home didn't have what she was looking for, but neither did the world.

Knock, knock, knock, knock, knock.

I hoisted myself onto one side and tried to sit up. My head spun. My hand must have shaken as I reached for the water glass. I took a sip and my insides swayed. There was nothing to do but sleep it off. For some people, this would be one of those I'm-never-drinking-again-type hangovers. For me, it was Tuesday morning. Or was it Wednesday?

Get the door.

The knocks came faster, closer together, until they caught up to the pounding inside my head. I collapsed onto my back, waited for the nausea to settle, and let the dull, insistent rhythm lull me to the brink of sleep.

Tap, tap, tap.

The sound had moved. It was coming from the window now. But I was pretty sure I was dreaming. Or maybe I was still drunk.

"Tom?" a voice called.

Oh, man. It was her.

"Time to get up!" chirped the voice in the teasing, singsong way I remembered from childhood.

I kept my eyes sealed shut. I pictured a clear, still pond inside me. If I concentrated hard enough, I could block out her voice and keep the bad stuff down at the soft, muddy bottom of the pond, where it belonged.

Tap, tap, tap.

Focus. Forget the tapping and calling. Keep the bad stuff where it belongs so the few relationships you have left don't blow up in your face. So your hands stay down at your sides instead of wrapping around someone's throat. So you don't explode in rage or start to cry and never stop.

There. Pond secured. Crisis averted.

Somewhere between asleep and awake, the tapping grew dim, and my thoughts drifted back twenty years, to a blue house that stood on top of a sloping hill on a leafy, tree-lined street. In the back of the house was a wooden deck. Because the house was built on a hill, the rise of the deck created a three-foot opening beneath it. It was filled with smooth gray and white stones, like a secret landscaping project someone had started and then abandoned. I'd crouch down and crawl beneath the slats of the deck, searching for the best stones. I'd pick up the smooth ones and rub their cool, flat surfaces across my cheek like my dad showed me to do during trips to the beach in Door County. Gliding those smooth stones across my cheek was a way to commune with nature, to become one with the elements. When I nuzzled my cheek with those stones, I became smooth and cool, too. When I breathed in the fresh breeze, I became light as air. When I was outside, in nature, I felt free.

Sometimes I'd get so absorbed in my imagination, I'd forget I was beneath the deck. I'd stand up suddenly and whack my head on the wooden planks above. My head would throb and I'd wail and scream until someone came to acknowledge my pain. And that's how I started to become an American man. *Suck it up, buttercup,* said the grown-up. *You're fine.* Real men don't cry. Real men don't feel. Real men bear the pain with dry faces and raised chins, their emotions broken and corralled like horses. Maybe that's why the tears still hadn't come. Not since that day, somewhere on the outskirts of Mosul, when a series of 7.62-caliber rounds exploded skull bone into a golf-ball-size crater, and my squad leader, Sergeant Diaz, was suddenly gone forever.

"Hey, Tombo. Wake up. We gotta go."

My sister, Beck, was standing outside my window with her forearms pressed between the sill and the frame. She spoke softly, like she knew about the bad stuff at the bottom of the pond and didn't want to stir it up. She was saying something about a doctor's appointment. Something about therapy. Something about how today was *the* day, and that I'd promised her I'd finally go talk to someone. Talk about what, I didn't know. I was fine.

I survived the war, got outta the army, and like my grandfather before me, I hit the ground running. Bampa had used the GI Bill to go to law school and start a family. I'd rented an apartment, gotten a job, and used mine to enroll in firefighting school. It was all going well. I was really happy about it. Overall, that is. I mean, sure, you couldn't expect most employers to understand how military experience translated to civilian experience, right? So maybe the jobs I'd had since getting out of the army weren't quite the right fit. But you gotta start somewhere.

I'd been trained to make split-second, life-and-death decisions that determined whether or not other human beings lived or died. So what do you do with me when I come home? Well, you could put me in charge of something important like keeping drunk people off the main stage at the state fair. Make me stand there in the wee hours after the fairgrounds have closed, when the last few drunk stragglers are searching for cars they shouldn't be driving, just in case they climb up on the stage and try to mess with the sound equipment. If they climb up onto the stage, I'm your guy. I'll be there to put a stop to it.

Or maybe I'd be good at pacing the long, carpeted corridors of the Hyatt Hotel between the hours of 10:00 PM and 6:00 AM, or staring at the blinking screens of thirty-two security cameras in the basement office of that hotel as they record absolutely nothing for hours on end. I could be really good at something like that, too.

Okay, maybe my part-time, third-shift job at the Hyatt was a step or two backward, career-wise. I wasn't outside, communing with nature, but at least I could walk up and down the hallways sometimes. At least I wasn't stuck in a cubicle or inside an armored vehicle. I could *move*. And hey, at least I *had* a job. That was more than a lot of vets could say, right? I had a job and a place to live. At twenty-three, I rented a room in a three-bedroom apartment with a couple of eighteen-year-old college freshmen because my drinking habits complemented theirs. It was a good setup. I'd buy them Carlo Rossi wine — the alcoholic grape juice in gallon jugs with the little glass handles. As long as I kept them buzzed, they didn't seem to notice or care about my increasingly frequent trips to the bar to get blackout drunk.

On weeknights I'd go to the bar because it was how I was keeping myself together. In the days and months and years after war, the simplest things threatened to stir up the past. A car parked on the side of the road that could blow up at any second. An invitation to see a movie in a theater I couldn't enter without having a panic attack. The red-and-white scarf of a party guest who morphed into an insurgent before my eyes.

But even with all those triggers, going out in public was more tolerable than being alone. Something was gnawing at me from the inside, something I couldn't quite put my finger on. It wasn't just panic attacks and flashbacks. It was something else I couldn't explain. Something I vaguely sensed but didn't understand. This thing, whatever it was, amplified the noise inside my head. It was like listening to a tape of recycled thoughts on repeat.

It was your fault.

It was your fault.

You should have been there.

The triggers out in the world were easier to withstand than the thoughts and memories in my mind. I found that I could drown out the noise in my head by distracting myself with some other kind of noise. Like a noisy, crowded bar, for instance. That was usually loud enough to blot out the memories of the noise of Mosul. And if the noise in the bar wasn't enough to drown out the sound of car bombs, I'd shoot enough Car Bombs until I couldn't hear shit.

"We gotta go," said Beck. "We're gonna be late for your appointment."

What did an appointment matter when life could be taken from you any second, even if you didn't deserve to die? You could die *just like that*, even if you were really young, or a really good guy, or had a wife and kids. That was the reality of it. And so it didn't really matter if I was late to an appointment, or missed an appointment, or left Beck standing outside my window for hours on end. It didn't matter if I pounded shot after shot after shot. Or if I took a few Ambien before going out drinking. Or did a little cocaine in the bathroom of the bar, or took some Special K, just to see what happened. Because whether I lived or died was out of my hands, anyway.

And it's not like I was trying to get drunk or high for fun. Once I'd muted the noise in my head with the noise of the bar, getting drunk or high was the only way I could sleep. Ever since I got back from Iraq, I couldn't sleep for shit. If the booze and drugs didn't make me pass out, the sheer exhaustion of filtering that much poison through my insides would eventually knock me out by morning.

I knew exactly what I needed to handle the triggers and

keep the bad stuff down where it belonged. I was just a little sleep deprived, that's all. Especially because now, when I was finally exhausted enough to get some sleep, my sister was standing outside my window, yammering about a goddamn doctor's appointment I didn't need to go to.

"Go away," I said. "I'm fine."

Silence.

I lay frozen in bed like a deer who senses the hunter. Then, in the long silences that drifted in from the open window, I found the space to finally drift back to sleep. I slipped gratefully into that warm, peaceful state of relief. A place without a past or a future. The euphoric pull of nonexistence, where I could finally and forever forget what happened.

As long as she wasn't still standing at my window. The thought jolted me awake again.

She wasn't still standing there, was she?

My heart beat faster as I lay in bed. I could feel the bad stuff rising up. She needed to leave.

When Beck had first brought it up, the whole talking-to-someone thing, I'd put her off as long as I could. It wasn't too hard. I'd just told her, sure, I'd go to therapy. But the therapist had to be a veteran.

"No problem," she'd said.

"A *combat* veteran," I'd insisted.

"Okay," she'd frowned, less sure.

"A combat veteran who was deployed to Iraq. And in this century, too. Not, like, during the Gulf War," I said.

That shut her up — at least for a few weeks while she conducted her search, like an amateur detective. She called psychologists in private practice. She scoured government websites. She spoke with administrative assistants and grad students and doctors.

"Do you have anyone on staff who's an Operation Iraqi Freedom combat veteran?" she'd ask.

Then, one day, someone on the other end of the line actually said yes.

"Tombo," she said again, breaking the silence with my childhood nickname.

"GO THE FUCK AWAY!" I roared.

That should have done the trick. It was ironic that I'd become a warrior in a global conflict because my loving, generous, honorable family of origin is possibly the most conflict-averse clan on the planet. Battling head-on and surveying the aftermath just isn't in their nature. They're so damn sweet and so petrified of confrontation that they'll leave things unsaid forever rather than have a brief but potentially uncomfortable exchange. Growing up, fights would often be followed not by a conversation but by a painstakingly crafted letter slipped under a bedroom door. The reader of the letter would emerge to give the writer of the letter a hug, which meant all was forgiven and the whole thing was over, never to be talked about again. Sometimes I wonder if the war I made, and the war that my grandfathers and my ancestors made, was just the expression of a million tiny conflicts that were stuffed down through generations instead of brought to light. Maybe that's all war is, anyway — people who don't know how to handle conflict finally handling it the only way they know how.

So there was no possible way that my sister, with that same nonconfrontational DNA, would stay at my window after I'd told her, point-blank, to go the fuck away. She'd shrink like a violet and leave. The next time I saw her, she'd throw me a little shade at first, but then she'd pretend it never happened.

"Tom," she repeated.

Her voice was strong and gentle, like waves against rocks. Like she was perfectly willing to erode my will over thousands of years.

"Come on. It's time to go," she said.

I sat up again. All the way up this time. I don't know why, but I reached for my shoes and put them on. I stood up and almost puked. I walked out the door and down the steps of my building.

Dark clouds hung low and depressed above faded brick storefronts and pointed rooftops. The wet, soupy remnants of fallen leaves clung to gutters and congregated along the curbs. Tangled green weeds sprouted from the sidewalk cracks. The lingering fumes of alcohol in my lungs were replaced with fresh air that rolled in off the lake from ten blocks away.

I never minded the ordinariness of the city, its age, the way it lingered, almost purposefully, between having once been great and having the potential to be great again. Between the corner bars, above the rough, worn streets, beyond the freeways and the lone, tall skyscraper, were forests and farmland and fresh air and a lake that stretched across the skyline like the sea. On good days, the fresh lake air traveled inland, energizing the city and bringing its citizens to life.

That day, the sky was a gray dome holding the world together, holding me together somehow. It seemed big and absorbent above me, like it could take anything I offered up to it, like it was big enough to swallow the past.

I took a deep breath in, exhaled, and climbed into my sister's car.

2

WHAT HAPPENED

The administrative assistant looked nervous. I don't remember what the rest of her looked like, but I remember her nervous smile when Beck and I first walked into the office. She asked us to take a seat. Then she knocked on a door, opened it a crack, and exchanged low murmurs with someone we couldn't see. We were late for my appointment, but it wasn't too late. The guy would still see me, she said.

Beck had found an OIF combat-veteran-turned-social-worker and booked an appointment for me because she was a doer. A maker. A producer. She'd just written, produced, and starred in a short film. The film was about a woman whose roommates turned out to be figments of her imagination. There was this scene in the film where the main character tried to slit her wrists in the shower, but one of the roommates — the guardian-angel roommate, I guess — stopped her from going through with it at the last second. I couldn't decide if Beck was afraid I was going to kill myself, too, or if she just really wanted to be my guardian angel. Maybe both.

In the waiting room, we waited in silence. I was ready to tell the social worker I was fine. I just needed to get out in nature a little more. The short walk from my apartment to Beck's car had perked me up and given me some relief from my hangover. Being outside awakened the senses, which seemed to dull my pain. If I could focus on the wind against my skin or the scent of crushed leaves, I could temporarily forget about what happened in Iraq. If I could just be outside, where there was enough room to move, I could move past what happened back then.

That's what I'd tell the social worker. The thing about nature. If I told him I blocked out the noise in my head with the noise of a bar, he'd probably make me go to AA. The nature thing sounded better. Less alcoholic. I'd go with that. I just really, really hoped he wouldn't ask some lame question like, "What seems to be the problem?" I couldn't stand stupid questions like that.

A white guy in his midthirties emerged from behind the door and stepped into the waiting room.

"I'm Jack," he said, reaching to shake my hand. "I'm a clinical social worker," he said.

Jack's dark hair was carefully coiffed in a large, deliberate pompadour that stretched past his forehead like a plant seeking the sun. It seemed like his sole attempt to remind the world he was once young and hip. The rest of him had settled into the safe mediocrity of middle-aged, middle-income Midwesternness: nondescript brown shoes, sensible slacks, suburban physique, and a perfectly pressed button-down shirt his wife had probably ironed that morning. But it was clear Jack had an agenda. There was an outcome he was after. I didn't know what it was, but I could tell just from shaking his hand that he knew exactly how to get it, no matter how unassuming he looked at first glance.

My dad was a social worker for thirty-two years. When I first toyed with the idea of following in his footsteps, he told me there were two kinds of social workers: the kind who genuinely wanted to help people and the kind who were so messed up, they needed an entire career to figure out why. For the latter kind, working through other people's problems was just a way to poke and prod into the hairy folds of their *own* trauma. They used client sessions as therapy sessions, either projecting their own issues onto the client or using the client's issues to distract themselves from their own problems. I had an idea which type of social worker my dad thought I'd be. I wondered which type Jack was.

"Would you be more comfortable if your sister was in the room?" Jack asked, ushering me toward his office door.

Beck leaned forward in her chair, wide-eyed and eager, hoping I'd say yes — like my mental health was an item she could finally check off her to-do list.

"No, I'm good," I reassured everyone, including the nervous assistant. She and Jack seemed to think I was there against my will — like Beck was the only thing stopping me from running out of the room and into oncoming traffic. But besides what remained of my hangover, I was fine. I was at the appointment of my own free will, and more important, I didn't *need* to be there. I was just there as a courtesy to Beck, since she went to all the trouble. She wanted me to talk to someone, so okay. I'd talk. I'd tell Jack that I was a functioning, contributing member of society and that I was fine. More than fine. Why did everyone seem to think I wasn't fine?

I left Beck in the waiting room and followed Jack into his office. He sat down behind a big, outdated desk. I chose the empty office chair directly across from him. On the wall behind Jack hung framed photographs of him with his buddies in Iraq. Images of sunglasses, weapons, and fatigues had been lovingly framed and displayed like fancy medical degrees. If I were sitting across from any other social worker in town, it'd be impossible to explain the unspoken things captured in those photographs of war.

"So," said Jack, and paused.

I waited for him to ask one of those shrink-ish questions you hear on TV, the kind that made me cringe. "What seems to be the problem?" was only slightly worse than "What brings you here today?" Maybe, if he asked that, I'd say something snarky, like "My *sister* brought me here today." But Jack just looked at me for a moment without saying a word.

Finally, he asked, "What happened?"

I stared at him for a moment, completely taken aback.

What happened?

The question inserted itself into my chest like a key into a lock.

What happened.

Those were the two words no one had dared ask until that moment — two years since I'd returned from twelve months in Iraq, where I'd served in a scout sniper platoon as part of Operation Iraqi Freedom. Those were the exact words I couldn't stop asking myself.

What happened.

What happened to me?

Tommy Voss. Tombo. I was the kind of guy who was friends with everyone in high school. I was the quiet one, but when I spoke up, everyone laughed at my jokes. I was a lover, not a fighter: a lover of football and video games and after-school snacks and Kimmy. She was a wicked basketball player back then, all thin and tall and blonde and bright-eyed. We'd chat on AOL Instant Messenger when the internet was still in its adolescence, just like we were. On weekends, we'd get drunk on Smirnoff Ice.

When I was away at basic training, Kimmy mailed me letters and photographs. The raciest pictures were of her and her friends at the beach in their bikinis. I put the pictures up in my wall locker in our barracks. The guys in my platoon would crowd around the pictures and call to their friends, "Dude! Go check out Voss's locker! He's got all these chicks!"

But I only had one. It was her.

Kimmy was the kind of girl who'd fly 1,991 miles just to spend forty-eight hours with me right before I deployed to Iraq. And then, after saying goodbye to me in a Seattle hotel room and letting me go so bravely, she kept visiting my mom the whole time I was at war, just to make sure Mom was okay.

For better or worse, leaving Kimmy to join the army and go to war felt as natural to me as breathing. My Bampa, my father's father, was a marine who fought in the battle of Iwo Jima. My maternal grandfather was a sailor who shuffled papers in London during the war. But my family wasn't a military family — they were a service family. They came to the United States from Ireland and Germany, Poland and England — white European immigrants who married other white European immigrants, and sometimes Native Americans. They were Catholics, bearers of children, teachers and social workers and volunteers. They were lawyers, but not the kind who made a lot of money. They were potato farmers who never missed Mass, veterinarians who accepted payment in trade, community servants who died in the care of the hospice program they'd founded.

In this family you were rewarded by thinking of others first. The more you gave up selfish desires for the greater good, the more you were loved and admired. The more you indulged selfish desires, the more you were disapproved of. It's pretty easy to understand if you break it down by career choice: teacher, social worker, volunteer coordinator, civil servant = good. Entrepreneur, hedge-fund manager, movie star, real estate investor = bad. It was okay to be poor, just as long as your poverty could be blamed on a noble career path and not laziness. It was okay to be successful, just as long as your success helped others first. It was even okay to make money, as long as it wasn't too *much* money, you donated most of it to charity, and you didn't go flashing it around like some kind of *rich* person. You could eat in a fancy restaurant as long as you volunteered at the food pantry, too. You could marry into money and attend the best law school if you used your degree to fight for social justice. You could trust that your service meant you were preferred in God's eyes.

It wasn't hard to follow in my family's footsteps. Examples of service — the sacrifice of it and the honor in it — were everywhere I looked. My mom began her career teaching emotionally disturbed children and kids with severe autism. A typical workday for my dad might include getting bitten by a handcuffed teenager or tackling a twelve-year-old boy to stop him from hurting his own mother. My Bampa had to leave his new wife, who was pregnant with their first child, to go serve his country in Japan. My grandmother spent every holiday season collecting donated gifts so poor families in her community could give their kids Christmas presents. The sacrifice and the selflessness of it all only became sacred when you rubbed at the bite marks, changed the ten-year-old's diaper, kissed the pregnant belly goodbye (maybe for good), or wrapped the hundredth gift for a stranger who wouldn't even thank you — all without a single complaint. You were most loved and admired when you carried your cross quietly, and with restraint.

I was born of that restraint. Staying with Kimmy would have been an emotional indulgence, like I was spoiling myself with something I didn't deserve. I had to deny myself, and her, the pleasure of too much happiness. I had to find something difficult, something punishing, something most people would complain about, so I could find the strength within myself *not* to complain about it. I had to find a way to be of service.

In the army, I found a way. I could serve my country, protect those who couldn't protect themselves, and preserve a way of life where people felt safe. I thought everyone deserved to feel safe, and I thought that ideal was worth defending. The army also paid for college when my parents couldn't afford to put both me and my sister through school. And if I needed one more reason to join, I had Bampa. He'd died just a few years before I left for basic training, when his heart finally surrendered to World War II battle wounds from fifty years earlier. Maybe joining the service and following in his footsteps would have made him proud. Maybe he would have understood.

Maybe he would have understood what happened.

What happened.

What happened to my friends?

My friends were the guys who stood by my side in the lush, open spaces of Kurdistan, watching big, sun-filled skies melt into rich reds and yellows and oranges. They were the ones who surrounded me the morning I emerged from the windowless Conex container where we slept and looked up to see thousands of blackbirds suddenly take to the sky, filling it like flecks of paint across a never-ending canvas. They were there, with me, before I *needed* the sky to be big, before I had any pain to offer up. They were there, with me, when it was beautiful.

My friends were also the ones who annoyed me, snatched cigarettes, talked trash over pirated DVDs. They were the ones who breathed and bled and sweated and stunk next to me in the cramped interiors of armored Stryker vehicles that rumbled through the cramped city of Mosul. They were the ones who leaned over me as I lay, unconscious, knocked to the floor of a moving Stryker by enemy fire. They were there when it was ugly. They were the ones who kept me alive.

What happened to them.

What happened.

What happened to my sergeants?

Sergeant Clark and Sergeant Diaz were our fearless leaders who flew bravely into battle, their limbs thrashing through the twilight, their weapons extensions of their limbs, their bodies dodging mortar fire like ninjas dodging blows, until suddenly they weren't anymore. What happened was they were saving lives one minute, being carried from vehicles the next.

What happened.

What happened was death.

The death of those who were hunted in the streets between smoldering burn pits, where breath turned to dust beneath a foreign sky.

The death of the person I used to be, who died there in the streets of Mosul with his friends and sergeants and would never come home from war.

The death of an ideal, carried down through generations and ending with me. What happened was I went to be of service, and I failed.

What happened was scientifically impossible, because matter can't be destroyed, it can only change form. But the scientists who said that were wrong, because what happened was the death of my soul.

But I didn't tell Jack any of that. After Jack asked his question, I said nothing. So he waited. He listened for the answer I couldn't yet give and left a space for it to appear.

In that space, something inside me that had been sealed shut and pushed down began to expand. It rose up and out, wracking my body with sudden sobs, like waterfalls. The sound of my sobs reverberated off the ceiling. Tears poured from me in a massive wave of grief and shame and sorrow, tears poured like alcohol, like all the shots I'd taken the night before were being filtered through my eyes. Tears poured like blood, ounce for ounce and pound for pound in lives taken and lost. There couldn't have been more blood in my veins than tears that poured from inside.

I cried because I hadn't cried before. Not once. Not since the death of Sergeant Diaz. I cried because I couldn't undo any of what happened. Because what happened would never, ever leave me, no matter how much I smoked or drank or kept it down or pretended it didn't matter anymore. I cried because there was no sky big enough, not anywhere in the world, not even in outer space, to absorb this much pain. I cried because Jack made it okay to cry. With the permission of his silence, the protective shield that had formed inside me in childhood, and hardened to titanium during war, liquefied and ran clear from my eyes. I wasn't fine. I wasn't fine. I wasn't fine at all.

The keening ended just as abruptly as it had begun. I sat with Jack in the silence. He waited a long time before speaking again.

"I'll see you back here on Friday," he said.

I decided then that he was the kind of social worker who really wanted to help people. I decided that his agenda was to help me.

"See you Friday," I said.

I meant it.

3

HEAD DOWN, PANTS ON

When inanimate objects hit the floor, there's a crashing sound. When human beings hit the floor, there's a thud. *Thud*. Private after private was yanked from his bed by drill sergeants who paced through our barracks like predators. They grabbed soundly sleeping bodies from top bunks and hurled them and their mattresses to the floor — a six-foot drop below. With every *thud* I said a silent prayer of thanks for my bottom bunk.

"Toe the fucking line!" shouted a drill sergeant.

Our entire platoon was up and in line in less than a minute. In my sleep-induced stupor, I tried to get a sense of the time. It was pitch-black outside and still hot as hell — that muggy, choking heat of a Georgia summer night. There was no air-conditioning in our barracks, so we toed the line in as little clothing as possible — physical training (PT) shorts or army-issued, shit-colored underwear.

Fort Benning was just outside the city of Columbus, about a hundred miles from the Alabama border. The average temperature in July was a punishing 92 degrees. Thick, still air hung above flat, wet plains that gave way to rolling hills — the perfect setting for grueling midday marches. With a forty-pound rucksack, a sweat-soaked uniform, and rust-colored mud that practically swallowed my boots with each step, marching in the Georgia heat was almost enough to make me regret joining the army altogether.

It was spring 2003, and I was about eight weeks into basic training — a thirteen-week boot camp to turn soft, selfish teenagers into trained killing machines. On March 19, 2003, just weeks after I'd started basic, the United States and its allies declared war on Iraq. The threat of being sent to war felt vague, distant, and less like a threat than a chance to put my training to good use. The possibility of war felt especially unimportant when two sour-breathed drill sergeants were screaming in our faces in the middle of the night.

We were in trouble for something. Big trouble. We had fifteen seconds to get fully dressed, downstairs, and into formation to hear about whatever we'd done wrong. It was an impossible order, and they knew it. We sprinted to our lockers and scrambled into PT uniforms amid a never-ending chorus of *Hurry UP Hurry UP Hurry UP Hurry UP Hurry UP Hurry UP Hurry UP.*

Ninety seconds later, a hundred and sixty privates from four different platoons stood at attention before eight fuming drill sergeants in the yard below. Every private from Charlie Company 2-19 had been pulled from his bunk in the middle of the night. On the rare occasions when we'd been woken up like this, it'd never been with the entire company. Someone must have fucked up big-time.

I made a frantic mental dive through the maze of the previous day, trying to remember if I'd screwed up. PT was fine — I was the third guy done with push-ups. I shaved and made my bed and put on the right uniform. I locked and relocked and re-*re*locked my wall locker. A few days before, I'd accidentally left it unlocked, and a hysterical drill sergeant had tossed the whole locker across the bay, my underwear and shaving kit flying like shrapnel, my tightly rolled socks rolling across the floor like severed heads. Even worse, our platoon had to do a shit ton of push-ups because of me, which was not the best way to make friends.

This wasn't about me...was it?

It couldn't be. I had the perfect temperament for military service. Head down. Mouth shut. The quiet one who was a good team player. I was like my dad, who dedicated his life to helping people who needed help but usually didn't want it. I was like my Bampa, who risked his life to protect the lives of the men he commanded during war. If called on to do something like that, I was pretty sure I'd be ready.

But not everyone came to basic ready to take one for the team. Like this kid from the Bronx, Ferraro. Where I kept my head down and my mouth shut, Ferraro kept his chin up and mouth open. He was constantly getting punished because of it. Ferraro was stumpy and muscular. He had straight, archless eyebrows that make him look like Bert from *Sesame Street*, and a silhouette of black stubble on his head that never quite disappeared, no matter how often he shaved.

Ferraro took a lot of pride in being the platoon clown

and didn't seem to care if it got him — or the rest of us — roasted. His favorite prank, the Pinkeye Nightmare, required a top bunk, a loose pair of pants, and a sleeping private. Ferraro would climb up onto the bunk, straddle the sleeping guy's face, pull down his pants, and shout "WAKE UP!" at the top of his lungs. When the sleeping private awoke with a start, the guy'd slam his face right into Ferraro's waiting asshole. Maybe, instead of a family who valued service and restraint, Ferraro hailed from a long line of court jesters or reality TV stars. Maybe, in his family, it was a sign of character to indulge in humor that only you found funny. Or maybe Ferraro was just kind of a dick.

As my eyes adjusted to the darkness of the yard, I noticed a private who wasn't standing in formation with the rest of us. Instead, he was standing apart from the entire company, as if he'd been put on display. He was surrounded by drill sergeants who leaned in toward the private like they were ready to pounce. In the darkness, I strained to see who it was. When one of the drill sergeants stepped away from their circle of shame, he revealed a private with a stumpy, muscular physique, straight, archless eyebrows, a silhouette of black stubble, and surely an anus clenched in fear.

It was Ferraro, the face sitter. The butthole bandit.

My heart did a little heel kick — this jerk was finally going to get what was coming to him. Then my heart sank — Ferraro was from my platoon. If Ferraro was going down, we were all going down with him.

"Cum stains!" shouted a drill sergeant.

In the darkness, the drill sergeant paced back and forth in front of Ferraro, his white skin gleaming against the blackness of the night. He looked like a ghost floating toward a condemned prisoner and spoke in sharp, infrequent barks, with pauses so long you could drive a truck through them. Drill sergeants lived for this type of shit.

"It SEEMS," shouted the drill sergeant, "that Private FERRARO here thought it would be a good IDEA to take a little midnight FIELD TRIP!"

Silence. No one moved. No one breathed. Ferraro's chin quivered above his heaving chest. In his hand he clutched a small, oblong object that I couldn't quite make out in the dark. He looked like he was ready to shit his pants, vomit, or both.

"Apparently, Private FERRARO thought it would be a good IDEA to sneak out to BRAVO Company," said the drill sergeant.

We were Charlie Company. Charlie Company was never allowed to leave our barracks without permission, and definitely not to sneak out to Bravo Company, and most definitely not in the middle of the night.

"APPARENTLY Private FERRARO thought it would be a good IDEA to help himself to a little midnight SNACK!"

A few audible groans rippled across the company. Ferraro's entire face rippled and twitched at the sound of them.

"SHUT THE FUCK UP!" yelled the drill sergeant.

He spat in Ferraro's general direction before continuing:

"PRIVATE FERRARO so desperately wanted a CANDY BAR, that he LEFT HIS BARRACKS PAST CURFEW, SNUCK OUT TO BRAVO COMPANY, BOUGHT HIM-SELF A SNICKERS FROM THE VENDING MACHINE, GOT CAUGHT BY A DRILL SERGEANT, LIED ABOUT

WHERE HE WAS FROM, RAN AWAY, and GOT. CAUGHT. AGAIN."

You have got. To be fucking. Kidding me.

The sergeant's white skin turned a familiar shade of purple in the dim light — it was the look they got when they were about to burst a blood vessel from screaming so loud.

"PRIVATE HOT DOG HEAD!" yelled the drill sergeant.

"Yes, Drill Sergeant!" shouted Hot Dog Head, so named for the rolls of skin that bulged at the nape of his neck and made him look like a human shar-pei.

"WHAT PLATOON DOES PRIVATE FERRARO BE-LONG TO?" asked the drill sergeant.

Hot Dog Head paused a split second too long.

"I CAN'T HEAR YOU, HOT DOG!"

"Private Ferraro is from First Platoon, Drill Sergeant!"

Silence. Forty stomachs instantly dropped, including my own.

"HOT DOG HEAD!" shouted Drill Sergeant.

"Yes, Drill Sergeant!" said Hot Dog Head.

"DO YOU THINK PRIVATE FERRARO'S BEHAVIOR TONIGHT WAS ACCEPTABLE OR UNACCEPTABLE?"

"Unacceptable, Drill Sergeant!" he said.

The sergeant paused for dramatic effect, priming his vocal cords for his speech's epic finale.

"Then why the FUCK did YOU let him go?"

Mercifully, he didn't wait for Hot Dog Head's sputtering response.

"YOU ARE ALL RESPONSIBLE FOR PRIVATE FER-RARO'S BEHAVIOR TONIGHT. THERE ARE FORTY PRIVATES IN FIRST PLATOON, AND EVERY ONE OF

YOU HAD THE CHANCE TO STOP PRIVATE FER-
RARO FROM LEAVING. BUT YOU DID NOTHING!"

Forty pairs of eyes sent invisible laser darts of hatred directly into Ferraro's body.

"SO YOU ARE ALL GOING TO GET THE DOG
SHIT SMOKED OUT OF YOU WHILE PRIVATE
FERRARO ENJOYS HIS CANDY BAR."

Another drill sergeant grabbed the candy bar from
Ferraro's sweaty palm, unwrapped it, and shoved it back into
Ferraro's hand. We all watched him take a bite and start to
chew. And that's when we heard the most despised words in all
of basic training:

"HALF RIGHT, FACE!"

"Half right, face" is a command to make a half right turn
while still in formation. It gives you just enough room to do
push-ups and other PT without bumping into the guy next to
you. The civilian translation of "half right, face" is "you're
about to get super fucked up."

Ferraro finished his Snickers bar. Then he did the only
thing he was allowed to do — he stood there, surrounded by
drill sergeants, and watched us get our asses kicked.

After hundreds of mountain climbers and what seemed like
thousands of push-ups, when we'd all been dissolved to quiv-
ering messes, we were finally released to go back upstairs to
continue our punishment.

My legs shook as I climbed the steps to our barracks.
Sweating and heaving, we gathered like exhausted sheep
around Drill Sergeant Velasquez, who was holding Ferraro
by the arm. Velasquez kicked a mattress across the floor of the
bay — Ferraro's for the night. Each squad would keep watch

over Ferraro so he didn't take any more field trips, go AWOL, or try to kill himself. Apparently, guys subjected to this level of public humiliation often became suicide risks or runaways. We'd watch Ferraro in shifts: Was it thirty minutes? An hour? I was so tired, even fifteen minutes felt like an eternity. Once our shift was done, the next squad would take up the watch, and we could sleep for an hour or so until it was our turn again.

My squad stood in a circle around Ferraro's bed. He sat on the mattress, his arms wrapped protectively around his knees, staring downward. No one spoke. The minutes that ticked by felt like centuries under the weight of my body. Ferraro's eyes started to close.

"Wake the FUCK up!" someone shouted.

More minutes passed. Ferraro began dozing again. I resisted the urge to kick him and kicked the mattress instead.

"If we're staying up, so are you," I said.

I have no idea how much time passed, but it felt like going to the DMV after running a marathon. When we were finally relieved by Squad 2, I collapsed into bed for an hour of sleep. Before I knew it, Drill Sergeant Velasquez was back with two other sergeants in tow; it was 5:00 AM and time for roll call.

"Get the FUCK up. Toe the line. Get into your uniforms because we're going on a ten-mile march. Not *you*, Ferraro. You come with us."

I don't know what they did to Ferraro that morning. A few days later he was back in our platoon like nothing had happened — except he was different somehow. For the rest of basic, he barely spoke to anyone. He kept his head down and his pants on and graduated with the rest of us. But his spirit was broken. His desires had been battered and forgotten, or at least compartmentalized, at least for now. To survive, he had to relinquish the pleasure of individuality, but also its pain and consequences. He joined us, finally, without resistance. Ferraro's candy bar was forever etched in my mind as a reminder of what it means to be a soldier — to be so connected to others that your personal desires don't matter anymore. To be so connected that you can say no to what you want because saying yes would suck for everyone else. Becoming a soldier meant becoming responsible for your actions and for everyone else's actions, too. It meant you shouldered the burden of another's punishment as if it was your own. It meant you suffered shared pain and connected with others through the bonds of that suffering.

That's what it was, then, to join the army: to relinquish yourself completely. To let go of your wants and needs and succumb to the will of the whole. To willingly attend your own funeral, step into the casket, and inhale the scent of fresh earth as it was shoveled onto your beating heart. And to be reborn as a single cell in a giant body. To support without thinking, to act without questioning, and to defend the greater body with your life.

4

MAKE WAR, NOT LOVE

I was standing in a hotel corridor in a Holiday Inn in Seattle. I raised my fist to knock on the door in front of me, but my hand just hovered there. Kimmy was on the other side of the door. She was probably still in her underwear, or maybe just a T-shirt, maybe *my* T-shirt, I'm not sure. I was supposed to be inside the room with her.

Kimmy had flown from Milwaukee to come stay with me for a few days before I was deployed to Iraq. We'd been dating for two years by then. For most of that time, I was away at basic training or stationed at Fort Lewis in Washington State. She was back home in Wisconsin, brightening up our homeland, busy with college classes or work. As I stood outside that hotel room in Seattle, I could picture her back in Milwaukee — smiling at a friend or throwing her head back to laugh at a joke, even if it wasn't that funny, just to make the joke teller feel good. I could see my '98 Honda Civic in her parents' garage, stored out of the way and off to the side, like a high school yearbook you keep in a souvenir box in the closet. I could see her dad starting the car and running it once a month or so, every month, until I returned. So I'd have wheels to pick her up for dates when I got back. So I could pick right back up where I had left off. Most of all, I could see Kimmy waiting patiently for me to grow up and into the man she wanted me to be. A man ready for marriage and children.

We had forty-eight hours — maybe less — to pretend I wasn't about to be dropped into a war zone. My platoon was headed for Mosul, which would later be considered one of the deadliest battlegrounds of the conflict. The funny part was, at the time I was relieved not to be going to Baghdad — Mosul, in the north, seemed safer somehow. But wherever that military transport dropped me, it was go time. This was what I had trained for.

In the hours that were supposed to be filled with sex and dinner and drinks and one-last-times, the part of me that would've enjoyed those things retreated. Someone else rose up in his place. He was a warrior going to war, and his duty consumed him. With a quiet compliance that startled me, love stepped aside to make way for the forthcoming battle.

Kimmy and I sat in that hotel room until our time together turned from days to hours. I couldn't just sit around and watch the hours become minutes. I couldn't stay there with her another second. I had to move. I had to get outside. I needed air and sky so I wouldn't suffocate.

Someone watching us would have looked at me and seen a twenty-year-old kid and a leggy blonde in a hotel room and thought she was some kind of conquest for me. They'd have seen the way I quickly dressed while she lounged on the bed in various states of undress, hoping I'd change my mind and stay with her for a few more hours. For one more hour. For a few more minutes? The someone watching us would have projected something about my fear of commitment or intimacy or about boys being boys. But it wasn't that I wanted to keep my options open or sleep with other girls. I had to leave because I had to get on a plane to Iraq, and there's only so much adrenaline a human body can make. There's not enough to make love and war. To make war, you have to leave the love behind.

I packed furiously. I told Kimmy no, I couldn't stay, not even for a few more minutes. I had to go. She said the same thing she'd say later, whenever I'd blow her off out of the blue.

"I understand."

She turned her blue eyes from mine, smiling sadly. I knew that smile. It meant she hadn't given up on me yet. She still believed her perfect love might be enough. Like her smile or her kiss or her touch could keep a part of me innocent forever, no matter what I did or saw over there. She wanted to hang on to all of me, but she'd settle for keeping just a piece. I hadn't stepped a boot on Iraqi soil, but already I wouldn't — I couldn't — give her that. Not even that.

I kissed her quickly, stepped out of the room, and shut the door. I took a few steps toward the stairwell, turned around, walked right back to the door, and stood outside the room. I raised a fist to knock for her to let me back in. The sound of her sobs beat against the door from inside. I stood there and listened to her cry. I lowered my fist, walked down the stairs, got into the truck I'd borrowed to see her, and drove away. I drove back to base so I could get ready to get on the bus that would take us to the air base that held the plane that would fly me to war.

On the bus, I realized that the *I* that had loved Kimmy was now part of a *We*. We had first started to take shape in basic training. Now, hours before war, We were fully formed. Indivisible. And so it was We that left Kimmy in the hotel room that day. We flew from Fort Lewis to Maine to Ireland to Germany to Turkey to Kuwait. Kuwait, so named because it's where We had to wait, and wait, and wait for the sound of our C-130 aircraft to Iraq to cut through the silent night and drown out the memory of Kimmy's sobs.

5

RULES OF ENGAGEMENT

When the dump truck starts speeding up to the tail end of your convoy, you'll ignore the fear that rises in your throat. You'll repress the memory of the last dump truck you saw — the one that had a five-hundred-pound bomb in the back of the cab. You'll resist the urge to take out the driver immediately so he doesn't take you out first. You'll instead follow the rules of engagement (ROE). These rules will help you make decisions about whether to use force or engage the enemy. They'll offer a framework for making moral calls that would otherwise be impossible to make.

Because you'll be following the ROE, you'll fire a warning shot into the air. And when the driver doesn't stop, you won't panic. You won't think. Because you'll no longer be you, and the old rules of the old you will no longer apply. Three shots to the tires, and the truck will still rumble down the road. Two shots to the engine block. The truck will not stop. By that point, you will have followed every rule. By that point you'll be ready to engage the windshield to take out the driver. Then you will do just that. Then the truck will veer to the side of the road, hop a curb, and grind to a rolling stop.

And when you're first on the scene, and both doors are locked, you'll smash the passenger-side window and find the driver slumped over the steering wheel. You'll see that he's been shot three times — twice in the chest and once through the hand. You'll watch the medics struggle to get an IV in because the driver's veins have collapsed. You'll realize that one of the warning shots to the truck traveled through the engine compartment, blew through the driver's palm, and exploded out the back of his hand. He couldn't have shifted gears to stop the vehicle if he'd wanted to. You'll realize there are no weapons, no explosive devices, absolutely nothing in his truck. Later you'll think he probably wanted to stop but couldn't. Or maybe he wanted to die. Or maybe his truck was just too loud, and he couldn't hear your warning shots in the first place.

"Why the fuck didn't you stop?" you'll ask the man.

You'll watch as he's pulled out of the truck and onto the ground, gasping for air — survival breathing. You'll help try to seal his chest wounds.

You'll try to save his life. You'll watch your sergeant, SFC Long, saunter up to the truck.

You'll hear SFC Long sigh impatiently.

"Are we done here?" he'll say.

You'll park your vehicle a block away from the hospital, beyond the cement barricades that have been installed to prevent car bombs. You'll run behind the dying man as he's carried toward the hospital on a stretcher. His body will bounce up and down as you race past hundreds of civilians waiting in line for medical treatment. It will feel like you're in a parade no one wanted to come to.

All eyes will be on you. All eyes will shift, in unison, to your victim. All eyes will shift back to you, and you'll see that quiet flicker of restraint flash across each cornea: you'll see the human spirit reining in its own rage.

Suddenly, one of the guys carrying the stretcher will trip on a pothole in the road. Your buddy Ethan will trip and fall alongside him. The man will topple off the stretcher and onto the pavement in front of the huge crowd. His head will sound like a football helmet hitting the ground.

A hospital attendant will meet you at the entrance with a wheelchair for a man who will never again be able to sit up.

You will have followed the ROE. You will have followed orders. You will have followed protocol. You will have done nothing wrong. You will not think about the man in the truck until much later, when the war is no longer all around you but inside you, playing itself out over and over again. What will stay with you and haunt you won't be the man on the stretcher so much as the way your sergeant sauntered up to the truck and asked, "Are we done here?"

And those four words, with their cool, inhuman indifference, will wound you more deeply than the shots you fired that day ever could.

But you won't be able to think about that while you're still there. The man who drove the dump truck will die. You'll still be alive. And if you do as you're told — if you surrender yourself to the group until there's no telling where your boots end and someone else's begin, with no telling where your soul ends and another begins, no telling if you even had a soul to begin with — maybe you'll stay that way.

6

HAPPY PLACE

I rode the elevator to the sixth floor of the giant cinder-block building and walked along filmy white corridors beneath the hum of fluorescent lighting. I was ushered into a square room with a single window. Dr. Campbell, a military psychiatrist, was waiting for me behind his desk. He reminded me of that bald guy who ripped Tom Cruise a new one in *Top Gun*. It was as if they hired him just because he looked the part — late fifties, fit, six feet tall, with a buzz cut and a chiseled jawline. He'd been an officer in the army and, later, the navy. While he treated combat veterans at the VA and in combat zones, his background was in child psychiatry. Jack had arranged the appointment for me. I'd woken up on time and driven myself there. I owed it to Jack and Beck, if not yet myself, to make my best effort at getting some help.

Dr. Campbell gestured to an oversize chair. I sat in it with my back facing the window. He peered at my file, frowning. Whatever Dr. Campbell asked me, I was ready. Just as long as it wasn't, "What seems to be the problem?"

"What seems to be the problem?" he asked.

Before I could answer, he started asking more questions, one after another, like he was reading from a checklist.

No, I can't sleep. Yes, I drink. One, maybe two nights a week. No, I'm not lying about how much I drink. Yes, I think about killing myself. No, I haven't made a plan. Yes, it's clear from your tone of voice that you have seventy-nine other veterans you're responsible for besides me.

Dr. Campbell calmly pointed to a picture of a cabin that was hanging on the wall behind his desk.

"See this? This is my happy place. Whenever I'm feeling down, I think of this place and I feel better," he said.

He looked at me expectantly, like a professor anticipating a student's grand epiphany. Like this technique — the Log Cabin Technique (LCT), I imagined him calling it — was kryptonite for any patient resistant to healing.

My jaw must have dropped, but I didn't say anything.

"Do you have a place like that?" he asked.

I stared at him. Was he asking me to *find my happy place?*

"No," I told Dr. Campbell, "I don't have a place like that."

Dr. Campbell scratched something on a pad with his pen. Log cabin does not make veteran happy. Log cabin seems to make veteran angry. Veteran needs to be stabilized.

Dr. Campbell started to rattle off names of medications. Zolpidem. Trazodone. Antidepressants. Antianxiety meds. He wrote them on a prescription pad and handed me the paper.

"Just don't drink alcohol when you start taking these medications, okay?" said Dr. Campbell.

Sure thing. Easy.

"Do you have anything else you'd like to say?" asked Dr. Campbell when he'd finished writing my prescriptions. I wondered if that question was part of his checklist, too. I said nothing. He looked at his watch.

"Are we done here?" he asked.

I stood up and walked out the door.

Jack nodded his head, hung up the phone, and sighed.

"Dr. Campbell says you need to be more *open* about your experiences during therapy," he said.

"Dr. Campbell is full of shit," I said.

"If you don't like Dr. Campbell, you can see someone else at the VA," Jack said.

"Fine," I said.

"In the meantime, why not try the medications he prescribed? They might help you sleep."

"I'll think about it," I said.

"And there's always medical marijuana," said Jack. "A lot of vets find relief with that."

"Yeah, already on top of that," I said, cracking a smile. "Not exactly medical, though."

"Oh, gotcha. *Okay*, then!" said Jack.

I got up to leave.

"Hey," he said. "Actually, when you come in for your next appointment with me, would you do me a favor?"

"Sure," I said.

"Would you mind bringing me an eighth?" he asked.

"Sure," I repeated. "No problem."

Jack was trying to take my pain away. The least I could do was do the same for him.

7

FAMILY TIME

Jack led me up the stairs, past his glaring wife, and into his bedroom. He guided me through the room and into the bathroom and shut the door behind us.

I'd transitioned into the care of the therapists at the VA, so I wasn't going into Jack's clinic as often. So it made sense that this time, when he asked me to bring him some weed, he asked me to bring it to him at home. And that felt like a step in the right direction. Smoking pot with a licensed clinical social worker was a step up, mental health–wise, from pounding shots at the corner bar. It was good for me to be around another combat vet. Someone who understood what I'd been through. Right?

"Come over and hang out," he'd said. "We'll chill, we can smoke. It'll be a good time."

I drove to his home in Elkhorn, nearly an hour southwest of the city. My beat-up Honda trudged along dark freeways that cut through frozen cornfields and farmland. I arrived at a two-story single-family home in the heart of Wisconsin suburbia in the dead of winter. It's the kind of place where cops and teachers drink Miller Lite during Sunday football games and take their kids to basketball tournaments at the YMCA. I rang the bell, and Jack opened the door. He led me through the kitchen, which opened onto a large, sunken living room. His whole family was there, sitting in the dark, watching a movie together.

"We're just gonna be upstairs for a bit," Jack told them.

His wife looked at me but said nothing. Maybe no one had told her, when they married, that in the holy military trinity of God-country-service, *family* was an optional fourth add-on.

As I greeted his family with a quick wave, something flickered inside me, then faded. It felt far away, like the soft thud of bass music pulsing from a distant car. It felt like something I used to know, something I used to be a part of. It felt like Saturday morning in the blue house at the top of the hill. It felt like the blue-gray tufts of shag carpeting in the living room, or the taste of raw cookie dough when my mom let Beck and me lick the bowl clean. It felt like begging for my friend to come over and play. Then the flicker became a sound, and I could hear my dad's voice telling me no, my friend couldn't come over right now. Because right now was family time.

Family time.

I couldn't look Jack's wife in the eye again. I was tumbling down a rabbit hole into another memory of my family. I was fifteen. I was sitting at the dining room table with my sister and my mom. My dad was standing over us, holding a handful of burnt, crumbling debris in his hand. He was so mad, his eyes were set to bulge out of their sockets.

"Are you kids smoking GRASS?" he sputtered.

Beck and I managed to swallow our laughter. *"Grass!"* we'd giggle later, laughing at the dated term for marijuana, which we called *weed,* or *pot,* but never *grass.* Beck and I seemed to agree, telepathically, that our only hope for survival was our mutual silence. She knew the weed wasn't hers, just like I knew it wasn't mine. But *I* didn't know if it was hers, and she didn't know if it was mine, and we didn't want to throw each other under the bus in case one of us was, in fact, guilty. Beck thought the weed belonged to a friend of mine. I thought it was probably her boyfriend's. We both looked down at the table and said nothing.

My dad waited, his whole body tense, for one of us to admit to our dark deeds. As the social work supervisor for the county, my dad spent his days with juvenile delinquents. He worked with social workers whose job it was to help families stay together and help biting, kicking, screaming, law-breaking adolescents stay out of jail. His worst fear seemed to be one of his own kids becoming the type of kid he worked with every day — the type of kid who stole cars and sold drugs and smoked lots and lots of grass.

My mom started to cry.

"I didn't bring children into this world," she wept, "to do *drugs.*"

After what felt like an hour but was probably only five minutes, my dad took the handful of grass, puts it in a ziplock baggie, and announced, "I'm taking this to the lab for testing."

The lab was the police forensics lab, which was located in the same complex as his office. The implication was that he knew people at the lab, and *boy, would we be sorry* when he got the results back and the results pointed to *grass*.

A few days later he got the results back.

The substance he had in his hand that day was a big dirt clod mixed with *actual* grass — the kind that grows on your lawn. It was not, to his great disappointment, marijuana.

He shared this news with Beck and me with narrowed eyes, like we'd pulled one over on him. Maybe we'd switched the grass with actual grass when his back was turned.

As I followed Jack past his snuggling family and up the stairs, the faint flicker of these memories began to shine brighter. Their glow was like a spotlight on a part of me I'd forgotten. It was the morality instilled in me by my parents, the morality that defined me before I went to war.

Family time is sacred, it said.

You shouldn't be smoking grass, it said.

You shouldn't be smoking grass during family time, it said. *Especially not someone else's family time.*

Upstairs, on Jack's bathroom counter, proudly displayed like a trophy, was a marijuana vaporizer. It had this giant bag that trapped the cannabis vapor so you could take long pulls and get super high. I took two or three long, deep breaths from the bag. About twenty minutes later, when we were done smoking, we walked downstairs. I'm not sure if I said goodbye to his family. I walked out the door, got into my car, and drove home, stoned out of my mind. I wondered who else Jack had had over in the middle of family time to do sordid things in the bathroom while the kids watched Disney movies downstairs.

8

CIGARETTES

Kimmy arrived at my apartment building after
the ambulance left but before I'd finished my last cigarette. My
hands were covered in blood. They shook as I took a final drag
and flicked the butt into the street, where my friend Connor
had been lying moments before. Kimmy stood in the light cast
by the streetlamp. She wanted to take me to the hospital, but
I just wanted the pack of cigarettes she'd brought me. I was
drunk. Connor was drunk. Connor's blood shone on the wet
pavement. It speckled the sidewalk like abstract art, the drop-
lets and splotches expanding until they pooled into a dark pud-
dle in the middle of the street. That's where Connor had been
lying when we tied a T-shirt around his arm as a tourniquet
and the wails of the ambulance grew closer. I'd stood over him,
watching him flop around on the ground like a fish out of water.

I'd been sitting next to Connor's girlfriend on the couch
upstairs. We were at a party at my friend's apartment. I don't

remember what we were talking about. We were drinking Jack Daniel's Old No. 7. The whiskey was harsh going down, oak and cheap charcoal. Had Connor cheated on her, or had she cheated on him? I couldn't remember. Was she prone to locking herself in the bathroom and threatening suicide if he left her? I think so. It was that kind of relationship.

Connor had been one of my best friends since freshman year in high school. Our core group eventually included Kimmy and her best friends, too. When I was in Iraq and had the rare chance to Skype with Kimmy, she'd usually be hanging out with Connor and our mutual friends. Because of the time difference, I'd mostly call when they were up late partying. It was Connor I'd see standing behind Kimmy on the screen. He'd be taking shots of Jägermeister and prancing around in someone else's super short denim cutoffs, letting his balls hang out the bottom for a laugh. It was Connor and Kimmy who'd squeal together drunkenly as our friends pulled them away from the computer screen, away from me, to go out to some bar. They'd say goodbye to me, shouting in the general direction of Kimmy's computer, distracted by whatever the night held in store. I'd sit in a tent on the other side of the world and log off the computer, as alone as I'd ever felt, the sound of their laughter ringing in my ears. Somehow, I felt just as left out now, back home at a party, as I did in those moments when I was far away.

Kimmy hadn't been returning my calls lately. It was hit or miss. When I got back from Iraq, she tried hard to make it work. She'd call and ask me to go for a walk. I'd say yes, then never show. Or I'd "forget" that I'd made plans with her and go out with my friends instead. She'd cry. We'd talk. We'd try again. But I couldn't seem to hear her cries the way I had before. I tuned them out to go to war, and I couldn't figure out how to tune in to them again. When she cried, the most I could do was *want* to feel something. But I just sat there, watching her hurt, feeling nothing. Then I'd ghost her again. And of course, as soon as she found the strength to give up on me, I wanted her back. I think things were over between her and the marine. But that didn't seem to matter. I was pretty sure she was gone for good this time.

The face in front of me on the couch grew blurrier, softer. Connor's girl. Should I tell her that the doctors at the VA had diagnosed me with PTSD? At my last appointment, there'd been a checklist on a table. I had to check some boxes on a piece of paper. Then, quite suddenly, I had PTSD. The diagnosis was supposed to explain everything. But it didn't. Not even my best friends, not even Connor, could understand what the PTSD diagnosis meant to me. I mean, he'd get it *conceptually*. He knew I was a different person than I'd been before the war. We could talk about flashbacks and panic attacks. But how could I make him understand what it was to finally be given an answer — *the* answer — that didn't even begin to answer my questions?

And where was Connor, anyway?

CRASH!

It sounded like a window shattering. All eight of us froze. Then a mad dash for the door and eight pairs of feet clomping down the two-story stairwell and scrambling into the street past shattered glass. Connor was lying in the middle of the road in a pool of his own blood. He moaned in pain like an animal.

"What happened?!"

He went to push the door open, he said. But the door he pushed was a pull. Later I'd think he must've been mad about something and punched through one of the glass panes in the heavy wooden door at the front of the apartment building. I'd think he was jealous because I was talking to his girlfriend on the couch. I'd think it was one more thing that was all my fault.

By the time he got to the hospital, Connor had lost so much blood that they couldn't give him painkillers or morphine or anything. He'd severed his bicep and nicked the artery that ran through his armpit. He'd need hundreds of stitches inside his arm, inside his body, and outside, too.

I texted Kimmy, my hands covered in his blood.

Connor's fucked. Have 2 go 2 hospital. Pick me up a pack of cigarettes?

It was the middle of the night. She got there in minutes. She even brought the cigarettes just as I was finishing the last one from my pack. Her car idled in the street as she waited to take me to Columbia St. Mary's to see our bleeding friend.

I took the fresh pack of cigarettes from Kimmy. I tried to light another smoke, but the lighter kept slipping through my fingers. I sat down on the curb with my feet in the wet street. I finally managed to produce a flame and inhaled sharply. Kimmy stood there, waiting for me. Always waiting.

Milwaukee may as well have been Mosul. Wherever I looked, no matter where I was, someone was dying in the street. The blood followed me across the world. I couldn't get it off my hands. I said nothing. I felt nothing. I thought nothing, except for the one thought that kept rattling around inside my head. I didn't think about Connor and the months and months of recovery he had ahead of him. I didn't think about Kimmy rushing to my side at a moment's notice, when I needed her most. It didn't occur to me that even though she'd ended things, she still loved me. What occurred to me that night, on the dark street wet with blood, was that Kimmy had brought me the wrong brand of cigarettes.

9

TAILSPIN

Jack couldn't stop yelling at fat ladies. Apparently, it was getting to be a real problem. My social-worker-turned-smoking-buddy had become my coworker at a veterans' non-profit in Milwaukee. After we'd smoked together at his house, I couldn't go back there. I stopped seeing him at his office, too. A year later, Jack walked into the Brady Street nonprofit where I worked because he was looking for a job. His button-down shirts were no longer pressed. He was thinner and had dark circles under his eyes. He had difficulty holding my gaze when we talked. Since I'd seen him last, he'd gotten divorced, left his job as a social worker, and started dating a stripper. He needed a job, but he also needed help.

At the nonprofit was a café where vets could connect over coffee and muffins. There were support groups and fundraisers and concerts to address issues like veteran homelessness and addiction. There were community organizations and representatives committed to helping vets understand and learn to live with the trauma they carried from war. The woman Jack yelled at was one of those community members, dedicated to helping vets in Milwaukee. Unluckily for her, she visited our offices on one of the rare days when Jack actually showed up for work.

When he met her, he just couldn't help himself. Jack just *had* to let her know that she was "too fat." And the fact that she was "too fat" made him fly into a rage that only he could understand. Or maybe he didn't understand it at all. I heard the woman had burst into tears during his tirade and that Jack just kept on yelling at her.

See, the problem with veterans helping veterans was that, like a social worker who's just as messed up as his clients, the people facilitating the support groups and therapy sessions at the nonprofit were also the people who needed them the most. There was me, with my PTSD diagnosis and drinking problem and wounded soul. I was still alive. I was holding down a job. But the thing that had been keeping me awake at night was still keeping me awake. I knew it wasn't just PTSD, but since I still wasn't sure what the problem was, I still had no clue what to do about it. And nobody else seemed to, either. Then there was Jack, with his irrational fear of cellulite and new tweaker persona. And let's not forget Ken, the guy who'd started the organization in the first place. He was a Vietnam vet and the first person in America to get acquitted for murder by claiming PTSD as his defense during a drunk-driving trial.

Then one day Sergeant Anthony Anderson walked into the nonprofit, all six feet four inches and 315 pounds of him. Anthony and I sat down in the open office space on the second floor, which overlooked bustling Brady Street below. I'd just been promoted to vice president of the organization. The operation was expanding, and we were opening another location in another town. We actually had the resources to hire another peer support specialist to help oversee the expansion. I remember because it was the first time I'd ever hired anyone.

"Hey, I'm Tom," I said, reaching up (and up and up) to shake Anthony's hand. "I'm the vice president."

"You don't really look old enough to be a vice president," Anthony said, looking down at me.

Anthony was a gentle giant of a man, with kind eyes that sloped downward at the outer corners, like a puppy's. His wispy curls framed a decidedly square head, and he was such a big dude that he had — no joke — 16 EE–size shoes. Anthony's mouth was set in a straight line, the perfect, ironic punctuation mark to his highbrow, deadpan sense of humor. We spent his entire interview swapping stories of our mutual deployments as if we were old friends. He was in the infantry, I was in the infantry. He deployed in 2004–2005, I deployed in 2004–2005. At no point did we discuss his work experience or qualifications. I hired him on the spot.

Where Jack had become fast-talking and impulsive, chain-smoking cigarettes down to the filter, disappearing for days at a time, and quite possibly sleeping in the office, Anthony was practical and levelheaded. When he discovered that Ken's fund-raising strategy amounted to "People will give us money because it's for a good cause," Anthony took over. He set specific fund-raising goals and developed clear strategies to meet those goals. He was always overprepared; he'd run through conversations in his head twenty-five times before going into any meeting.

Anthony's trauma manifested itself in quieter, more

introspective ways. While Jack would lash out and I'd drown the past in drink, Anthony would disappear into the remote darkness of his basement any time an emotion threatened to emerge from the past. He'd descend those basement steps in peaceful silence, his considerate attempt to distance himself and his ghosts from his wife and young daughter.

With Anthony on the team, I felt excited about work for the first time in a while. I felt like I was being of service. With Anthony's strategic mind and me on operations, I felt like we could really make a difference for vets in Milwaukee. Even better, I didn't feel so alone.

Jack peeled down Brady Street in a cold sweat. Our timeline was tight — we had to find a print shop that could do a rush order that day. We needed to get a banner printed for an event we were holding that night. On event days everyone got stressed out. But Jack's stress level seemed excessive, even for him.

"I've got to tell you something," he said.

He stared straight ahead, hands gripping the steering wheel, not looking at me. Suddenly, I was the therapist and he was the client.

"What happened?" I asked.

"Last night I got arrested for buying crack from an under-cover cop. Now I have to be an informant for the police, or I'll go to jail," he said.

Jack was a pilot tail-spinning straight into a mountain ridge with no way to pull himself back up. His training as a social worker didn't matter. His master's degree couldn't protect him. His knowledge of human psychology couldn't heal him. Not even a stripper girlfriend who left little piles of glitter in the crevices of his car seat was enough to quell the pain. Jack had an arsenal of tools to defend himself against this kind of meltdown. I didn't have the degree or training or experience he had. If someone like him couldn't handle himself, where did that leave someone like me?

10

I WASN'T THERE

"Are you ready?" asked the doctor.

"Yeah," I lied.

The doctor held a pink highlighter in her hand. She raised it and pointed it between my eyes, as if she was shining a flashlight during an eye exam.

"Follow my highlighter with your eyes," she said.

She started to move her hand from left to right and back again.

Anthony had recommended her. He'd been doing EMDR treatment with her and it was helping him, he said. Basically, you move your eyes around while talking about your most traumatic memories. Somehow, it's supposed to help rewire your brain so the traumatic memories become more like regular memories and no longer cause so much pain.

The invigoration I'd felt at work had distracted me from my thoughts for a while. But when the newness of working with Anthony had worn off, there was the past again, waiting for me. It had never really left. Work was a charade. My friendship with Anthony was just a Band-Aid to cover up the truth: living with myself, as myself, was hell.

But I'd made a pact with myself not to kill myself until I'd tried absolutely everything I could think of to get better. Hell, I'd even skip suicide altogether if I could just find a little bit of relief — even for one day. That was all I really wanted, after all — not a quick fix. Just a break from the torment. A sliver of light in the darkness. Just one day when I didn't want to blow my brains out — not consciously, when I was willing myself not to find a gun, and not unconsciously, when the pull of suicide existed beyond my peripheral vision, like the tug of a strong current I couldn't see. It was always there, even if I pretended it wasn't or found ways to cover it up. If I could experience life without that nagging tug of suicide, I could find my center again. Then the memory of those centered moments would help me hang on when it seemed like the undertow of pain was strong enough to pull me down and drown me. In those moments, I could remember those twenty-four hours of relief I'd had and hope that another good day would come my way. I figured an entire day of true relief could keep me alive for at least a year. Maybe two.

I followed the floating highlighter to the right, then to the left, then to the right with my eyes.

I liked this doctor. She, unlike the treatment, was gentle. We worked with the same memory at each of our sessions. She'd guide me as I shared the memory out loud.

"Tell me," said the doctor, as she did at each session, "about an event from the past that's been making you feel depressed."

I took a deep breath in. My eyes continued to follow the highlighter back and forth, back and forth. I was sitting in a room in the VA hospital in Milwaukee. But my spirit — whatever was left of it — was seven years in the past and 6,144 miles away.

"Most of our platoon was gone that day," I said. "They were out on a mission, but I stayed behind. In the morning, at the mission brief, I'd been given the day off, along with a few other guys. It was a noncritical mission. Our platoon was basically giving a group of Navy SEALs who'd just arrived in Mosul a tour of the city. We weren't required to be at full strength, and we needed room in the vehicles to take the SEALs along. So they had three or four of us stay behind.

"We had the whole morning and into the afternoon to do whatever we wanted until the rest of our platoon got back. So I did the things I usually didn't get to do, like go to breakfast and eat an actual meal. Go to the gym and actually work out. Go to the internet trailer and check email and communicate with people back home. Take a nap. Go to lunch. We didn't get to do these types of things on a regular basis. So when we did, we felt fortunate.

"It was getting late, and our platoon wasn't back yet. It shouldn't have taken that much time. It was a short mission. I remember the sun setting and wondering where everyone was. Just as it got dark, everyone pulled up in their vehicles. When they got out, they were silent.

"I remember following my team leader and my squad leader to their room. It was a huddle-up for our squad.

"Our squad leader, Sergeant Richardson, waited until we'd gathered around him. Then, he said, 'Clark got killed.'

"It was just dead silence. Sergeant Clark was our platoon sergeant. He was the leader of the whole platoon.

"The next day, we had to burn his…they had this trash bag from the medical team with his uniform and body armor and all the stuff that was on him when he got killed. We had to light a fire. We just burned his uniform because it was covered in blood.

"The ammo pouches and all that kinda stuff, Sergeant Diaz took everything down to the bathroom to scrub out the blood. I walked in and he was scrubbing the blood with a toothbrush and crying into the sink.

"So I wasn't there for it. And that's the problem. That I wasn't there," I said.

The gentle doctor set down her pink highlighter on the desk.

"Let's take a break," she said.

During the break, we sat in silence. For some reason, I prayed. I don't know who I was praying to, exactly. I guess nature or God or whoever would listen to make the feelings stop. Please. I'm begging you. I'll do anything if you just take these feelings away. I'll do anything if you just end this torture. God, please let it end. God, please let me die.

"Again," the gentle doctor said. "Tell it again," she said.

I stared at the tiny plastic sphere on top of the highlighter cap. I could barely breathe to get the words out.

"Most of our platoon was gone that day," I said, "but I stayed behind. I stayed behind and Clark got killed. We burned his uniform because it was covered in blood. We burned the only things that were left of him. I could have stopped it.

Maybe I could have saved him. And that's the problem. That I wasn't there."

"Again!" said the doctor.

"I WASN'T THERE. I WASN'T THERE. I WASN'T THERE. I WASN'T THERE. I WASN'T THERE!"

The doctor dropped her pink highlighter on the desk.

"Great work today," she said.

Now it was time to stand up, walk out of the room, and go home.

I stumbled along the corridors to the elevator bank, but I was still in Mosul, taken back and left there as if I was dropped in-country from a military transport plane, with no way to get home.

11

LIFELINE

Sometimes, if I was lucky, the phone would ring and it'd be my buddy Ethan on the other end of the line. He'd be calling me, like he did from time to time, just to check in. He made these calls to all the guys in our platoon — those of us who were left — like a mother hen checking in on her chicks.

"Tommy Voss!" he'd say, his voice glowing warm in the dark of winter. "How's it going, man? Just calling to check in."

"It's cold as fuck," I'd say. "Sucks, it's too cold to get outside as much as I'd like."

"Yeah? I'm outside right now — in shorts and a sweatshirt!" he'd say.

And for what had to be the seventeenth time, "You need to get your ass out to California, man. I keep telling ya!"

And then, like always, he'd ask — no, but *really*, man — how I was doing. I'd tell him about school, or whatever job I happened to be working, or whatever was going on or not going on in my love life. I'd tell him I tried that EMDR stuff, but it didn't work for me. He'd tell me about his job teaching English, his fiancée, and then, over time, his wife and son. He'd tell me about the guys in our platoon. What they were doing. Where they were working. Whether or not anyone had heard from them lately.

The facts about our friends, like Ethan's phone call itself, were ordinary. The mundane details of each other's lives were the things we clung to when we could no longer cling to each other. The bonds of brotherhood forged in war had been buried by civilian life, by time, by the heart's desire to heal and change the past — but they were still there. We'd probably never all be together again. And even if we were together, we probably wouldn't talk about what happened to us in Iraq, let alone what happened after we got home. But Cal just got engaged, man. Ayden Sanches had a kid. Babak's working at the Department of Justice, did you hear? And that's great, man. So glad you're back in school. I really think you're gonna finish this time.

We were still a *We*. The people who were there when I lost myself still existed. And if they still existed, if I could still connect with them through Ethan's careful reportage, there was hope I could find myself again, too. For a few minutes, a few times a year, there was hope.

12
MONOLOGUE

"There is hope. There is this great, great hope that a realm exists where I wouldn't have to feel this way anymore," I thought.

I'd usually be on the way to the bar when the monologue would start in my mind. It wouldn't take much to get me going. Maybe I'd drive by a bridge.

"That would be a good place to do it," I'd think. "As good as any other, really. It's good enough because the bridge looks high enough. It has to be high enough so if I jumped off, I'd die. This is not the kind of thing you want to do half-assed.

"What if I just whipped the wheels of my car on the freeway? No, I couldn't do that. I don't want to hurt anyone else. Maybe I'll just take my seat belt off and see what happens. Maybe I'll find an empty country road. Where no other cars will be. I'll drive myself into a tree. WHACK. Or I could OD on all those prescription medications the VA keeps sending me in the mail. But what if I take all the pills and I still wake up and just have to go to the hospital and get my stomach pumped? That would be a pain in the ass."

With the thoughts of suicide still grinding away in my head, I pushed a heavy door against a wall of cigarette smoke. It gave way, and I stepped across the sticky floor toward my regular spot at RC's, a dive bar on the East Side. *My* dive bar on the East Side. Denim-wrapped flesh poured over the sides of the ancient wooden stools that lined the bar. The pool table, with its beat-up felt and misshapen cues, had abandoned all hope of being used that night. It was a weeknight, so there'd be no darts, no venturing outside to the patio, no fierce games of *Golden Tee* with friends. Just me, the youngest person at the bar, and the rest of them — the other people who had stuff to drink away.

I climbed onto my regular barstool. It was warm from someone else's ass. I could smell the stench of cigarettes and stale beer in my beard. The bar was like my own version of *Cheers*. Everybody knew my name. And everybody knew not to talk to me after the ninth or tenth shot. There was no school anymore. There was no job at the nonprofit. I'd quit them both. They were getting in the way of my drinking. And I needed to drink to quiet the thoughts and to keep the rage down where it belonged. There were no more visits to the VA or therapy sessions with Jack — not in his office, not in his bathroom, not in his glitter repository of a car. Even my friendship with Anthony, who I'd kept in touch with after leaving the nonprofit, and the phone calls from Ethan couldn't keep me from diving down this old, familiar rabbit hole.

Shot.

The monologue continued.

"I can't shoot myself because maybe my mom might want to have an open-casket funeral and my brains would be blown to bits and my body would be ruined and I don't want to ruin my body for my family. I guess I'd have the same problem if I jumped off that bridge, though. But however I do it, it might be a way to get out of this. I could exist in that shadowy place where Clark and Diaz like to hang out, where their ghosts hover between my world and theirs, tempting me to join them.

"Or maybe they want me to switch places with them. Maybe, if I killed myself, I could give them a second chance at life."

Shot, shot.

There it was. That sweet spot, where the monologue drowns itself in drink and dissolves to silence. I was safe, right there, for the moment.

In spring 2013, two more combat casualties happened off the battlefield, two more platoonmate deaths that weren't included in the official death tolls of war. My friend Luke shot himself in the head. My friend Max was found lying in a recliner, passed away at age thirty-seven. His family said it was from natural causes. Because there's nothing more natural, more human, than seeking relief from pain. These things happened in threes, just like celebrity deaths. I felt this communal body — my body — on the brink of death, just as it had been in Iraq. It was time to stop the pain or perish.

Shot.

Shot.

Shit.

That was one too many.

As I sat on my barstool, a reel started to crank. There was

no audio. It was like an old-timey silent movie that started flickering behind my eyes. A military convoy of twenty Stryker vehicles thundered down a Mosul street. There was my vehicle, near the front of the convoy. There was me, standing up in the back of the vehicle, my feet on the floor and my head exposed above the air-guard hatch. There was my weapon, gripped tightly in my hands, pointed outward at an invisible enemy. There was another guy standing up with me in the rear of the vehicle, and a TC (tank commander) standing in the middle. The three of us scanned our surroundings for danger as the Stryker rumbled down the street. The rest of our squad was tucked inside the vehicle, sitting on the benches that lined its interior. It was the air guards' job to guard the 1.42 million–dollar vehicle and alert the rest of our squad to signs of trouble in the city. Being the air guard was so dangerous that we all took turns doing it.

Close-up on me in the air-guard hatch: tense face, furrowed brow, shoulders clenched in anticipation of another blast. I saw myself fighting the urge to duck for cover from the ghost bomb that hadn't gone off yet, the bomb I was still anticipating years later as I sat in the bar in Milwaukee, drunk, watching mind-movies from the past.

A man in black scrambled down the street past an open-air sewage system. Brown skin. Black beard. He was less than two hundred yards from my vehicle, dressed in a traditional black kurta. Civilian dress. The man turned, stared straight at me, then dove behind a parked car. My team leader's mouth started to open and shut in slow motion.

"R!" shouted the mouth.

"P!" shouted the mouth.

"G!" shouted the mouth.

Rocket-propelled grenade. My team leader started firing round after round at the man in black; then my head flew back like I'd been hit with a baseball bat. My helmet was shoved down past the bridge of my nose by a force stronger than gravity. My feet were swept out from under me, and my body collapsed through the air-guard hatch. I landed on the floor with a silent, sickening thud. Then everything went black.

I watched the medic checking my neck. I saw my roommate crouched above me, peering into my eyes, looking for signs of life. He turned to the medic and shook his head.

"He's all fucked up," he said.

Sergeant Henderson held his radio to make an internal call to the rest of the platoon. I watched him mouth the words, "Voss got shot in the head with an RPG."

The film flashed faster in my mind. There was Ethan in his vehicle. There was my buddy Cal in his. They kept firing their weapons. They'd heard Henderson's call over the radio, and they were both sure I was dead. There I was on the floor of the moving vehicle, surrendering to the sweet promise of death: no more war. No more blood. No more me.

Henderson got back on the radio. He paused, thought for a second, then said, "Yeah, Voss headbutted an RPG. But he's okay."

My helmet was totally fucked. The whole side was cracked, the desert camouflage ripped away to reveal the reversible army-green camo beneath it. The elastic band that held my goggles exploded off the side of my head, and I could see exactly where the RPG had hit me: about two inches above my right eye.

Hit me with your best shot.

Hit me. Another Rumple Minze.

Shot.

Shot, shot.

Fast-forward to me on base in Mosul, at the gym, lifting weights on my day off. Cut to me taking a nap. Cut to Sergeant Clark standing in the air-guard hatch at the back of one of our Strykers. Cut to the clear blue sky. Watch the rocket as it sails through the air. Watch as it hits the back of Clark's Stryker, right where an M240B machine gun was mounted. Watch the machine gun explode. See the shrapnel as it flies through the air. See it slice Clark's face and neck. Now watch him bleed out as they rush him to the med station. Watch his eyes, still open. He's still alive.

Now cut back to me. In bed. Asleep. Watch me sleep while he fucking dies.

Cut to his family.

Cut to his children.

Shot.

Shot.

Shot.

Shot.

Shot.

Through the blinking lights of the jukebox, past the dartboard and pool table, I thought I saw the ghostly figure of Sergeant Diaz heading toward the bathrooms. He flickered and disappeared from the bar. He reappeared in the movie in my mind, in Iraq, standing in the bathroom in the hours after Clark's death, when I'd walked in on him at the sinks. He was running the water to rinse the blood out of Clark's ammo pouches, but the water pressure wasn't strong enough to rinse them clean, so Diaz was using a toothbrush to scrub the stained canvas. He was alone, at least until I walked in, and weeping openly, his tears falling into the sink and mixing with the water and blood. I didn't say anything. I used the toilet and left.

Shot.

And there was Diaz again, just a few weeks later, being carried to the medic's tent after an ambush. He'd been shot in the head, and everyone in the Stryker was covered in his blood.

No matter how much I drank, my friends were still dead. And I longed to join them.

13

ENOUGH

On a weeknight in early May, I stood in Beck's tiny second-story apartment in the doorway between the kitchen and the living room, because I had something to tell her. Beck was sitting in the dimly lit living room in an old, worn easy chair — the biggest piece of furniture she owned because a couch wouldn't fit through the narrow entrance to her apartment. We were drinking some kind of sweet, pink wine. She'd offered it to me because she had no clue how much I really drank, or why. Over time, I'd gotten better at hiding the worst of myself from everyone except myself. There was no stereo in her place, no television set, no sound from the street below. Just the dull murmur of the neighbor's TV drifting up through the thin floorboards and the sad stories of failure in our respective pasts and present. I was twenty-eight. It had been ten years since I'd joined the army. I'd tried college and quit. I'd tried all sorts of therapy and quit. I'd gotten a good job at the nonprofit and quit. To make ends meet, I'd been working off and on that winter, cutting down trees in the bitter Wisconsin cold so I could breathe and move and be outside and not suffocate myself in malaise. I was still drinking most nights. Every second of every day, I wanted to die.

Beck was thirty-one. She was working as a freelance copywriter after returning from five years in Los Angeles. Her filmmaker hopes had been dashed to dust and she'd quit in a sudden desperate fit. She'd sold her furniture, jumped into her car, and driven across the country in the beat-up Civic I'd given her before she left. Now she spent hours, sometimes days, alone in her apartment, holed up in the darkness, working for ten, sometimes fourteen, hours at a time. In addition to the crushed Hollywood dreams, she was nursing the umpteenth heartbreak from the umpteenth douchebag she'd fallen for — and this time had made the mistake of working with professionally. For weeks she'd been drinking red wine and crying in the bathtub over the guy, the kind of guy who said, "Sorry, man, I'm just not there" when she told him she loved him.

And so we drank together, and laughed a bit, and shook our heads at the sad things that our lives had become. We'd been properly set up for success and happiness at every turn, but we'd turned into alcoholic losers. Where had it all gone south?

"At least you have this big, traumatic event to blame your life on. What's my excuse?" she asked.

"At least you've had some adventures," I said. "You've traveled your own path. Maybe I should try doing that, too."

"Like what?" she asked. "Backpack Southeast Asia or something? Go to India? Ooh! I've heard of this really cool pilgrimage you can do in Spain, the Way of St. James — "

"Too many people," I said. "I wanna go somewhere quiet, where I can walk and move and clear my head, y'know? Spend some time alone in nature."

"How about Door County?" she asked.

When I was a kid, our family vacationed in Door County, a northern Wisconsin peninsula surrounded by Lake Michigan to the east and Green Bay to the west. We stayed at my aunt's cabin in Gills Rock, the northernmost point on the narrow strip of land. If you're looking at a map of Wisconsin, and you look at the state like a mitten you'd wear on your left hand, Gills Rock is the tip of your thumb. (By the way, if you get nothing else out of reading this book, let it forever be known that Wisconsin — *not* Michigan — is the true "mitten state.")

My mom and dad would take Beck and me on these long, difficult hikes through the forest surrounding the cabin. At age six or seven my sense of timing was probably off, but it felt like those hikes took hours. The foliage was so thick, entering the trailhead felt like entering a dark tunnel, even on the brightest summer day. I remember the forest floor being carpeted with leaves, and how the trail would narrow in places and widen in others. We'd often have to climb over fallen trees and logs laid across the trail, which made it feel like hiking an obstacle course. Surrounding me in 360 degrees, like an organic IMAX theater, were northern white cedars and eastern hemlocks, white and red pine, tamarack and American beech and papery birch with bark I could peel off like snake skin. Even in spots where the trail widened to ten or twelve feet across, the first person passing through would get a face full of spiderwebs. We'd hike up a hill that felt like a mountain, then tumble downward, tripping over knobs and stones on the path. Then one final curve to the right, and through the slats of space between the trees, I could spy the still, clear water of Europe Lake. The leaves beneath our feet began to mix with soft, white sand. Then the forest gave way to a clearing that opened onto a small beach.

Tall reeds sprouted in thick clusters at the shoreline, creating a narrow path where I could wade into the water. Europe Lake was as warm as bathwater as it lapped lazily around my legs. It was perfectly calm and clear as glass, so clear we could peer down and see hundreds of tiny minnows nibbling our feet and ankles. Swimming there was a welcome change from the colder, rough waters of Lake Michigan. But the glory of those hikes wasn't finally getting to go swimming — it was that victorious, hard-earned moment when I'd emerge from the dark forest onto the bright beach. It was the moment when, after all those stumbles in the darkness, I finally stepped into the light. But the path that seemed arduous in childhood wouldn't be enough now. I needed a longer journey. I needed more time. More space.

"Not Door County," I said. "Not anywhere, actually. I can't stay put in one place. I want to move, just try and move past all this stuff."

The thoughts were coming faster now despite the drink. I didn't just have to move, I had to walk. I had to walk down some sort of path, like in Door County, but not in Door County. Because I needed the sky without a canopy, big and absorbent above me. And air, and space, and time. I needed to walk somewhere where time stopped, or maybe where it never began or ended. But when it did end, I'd be there, and I'd be different somehow. Ethan's face flashed across my mind. I saw him in the California sun.

"I think...I think I wanna walk across the country," I said. The words hung in the air like incense. Beck's eyes lit up. "Yes!" said Beck. "Do it!"

I told her Ethan kept inviting me to come out and see him in California. What if I actually took him up on the offer? I didn't know what was wrong with me, exactly, but I knew it wasn't just PTSD. And I knew I couldn't take it anymore. Since I hadn't been able to numb the pain, talk through the pain, or run from the pain, what if I walked straight toward the pain?

That's it! Let's look up the distance. It's 2,700 miles from Milwaukee to Los Angeles on foot. It would take me five or six months, I think. No cars, no support vehicles, no rides from anyone. Just my two feet, the open road, and the ghosts of the past who demanded to be dealt with. I'd be totally immersed in nature. I'd sleep outside under the stars. I'd dig my feet into the soil and be filthy and breathe in the fresh air until my lungs were brand-new. I would become the road, the trees, the earth. I would rub smooth stones on my cheek until I disappeared. I would offer up my past to the big, open sky until nothing hurt anymore.

All I needed was a great, great space I could move through. A space that would allow me to walk so far, I'd lose the ghosts and memories of war and constant thoughts of suicide somewhere between the mountains and the sea. Los Angeles was close to where Ethan lived and really damn far from Milwaukee. It was perfect. Walking somewhere as far away as possible would give me time. I needed the minutes, the hours, the miles piled upon miles, the endless time beneath the endless sky that ended at the endless ocean. Only a great journey to the sea across mountains and plains and deserts was expansive enough to absorb what I had inside me. Milwaukee to Los Angeles is a long, long walk. If that wasn't enough time and space to heal, nothing was.

I'd finish the journey at the ocean, in Santa Monica. Once, while visiting Beck in LA, we drove all the way to the beach from Pasadena. But when we finally got there, I was too anxious to get out of the car. This time would be different. This time, I'd step right onto Santa Monica Pier without a second thought. I'd walk past the Ferris wheel and souvenir stands and the Bubba Gump Shrimp Company. I'd lean on the railing at the end of the pier until I could see nothing but the sea. And when I looked at the sea, I'd feel an endless sea inside me, an expanse as great as the ocean. A whole, healed soul reawakened to life. A soul so big it was connected to everything and everyone. And it would be through that sense of connection that I'd finally reconnect with myself. I'd reclaim my place in the world of the living.

I didn't know what that meant or how to do it, but I felt the possibility within me like a tiny seed of potential. That seed held the promise of something more for my life. Something beyond mere freedom from pain. Something that, if given enough space and time, might even start to look like joy.

Part 2

MOBILE

One must be patient like the earth.
What iniquities are being perpetrated on her!
Yet she quietly endures them all.

— Sarada Devi

14

THE RUCKSACK

Anthony was in his car when he got my call.

"Hey, man," I said to Anthony. "Do you have a ruck I can borrow?"

"Probably," said Anthony. "Why do you need it?"

"Well, y'know how we never really had time to address stuff when we got back from Iraq? I think I'm finally gonna take the time. I'm just gonna do it. I have a friend out in California, a guy I served with. Ethan. I'm gonna walk out there to see him," I said.

Anthony was silent.

"And so if I'm gonna walk across the country, I'm gonna need a ruck," I said.

I could hear him thinking it through on the other end of the line.

"What if I went with you?" he asked finally.

The second he said it, I knew it was right.

"Yeah. Sure. That'd be fine," I said.

Even though I'd been thinking of this as a solo journey, the truth was I'd be much more likely to finish if Anthony came with me. He was a strategic planner. He'd think of the things that never crossed my mind. When you're out alone in nature, in the middle of a mountain range or desert, that kind of thinking and planning can save your life. And if I didn't have the strength to keep going on certain days, if giving up became a little too enticing, Anthony'd be there to help me keep going. Maybe, as Anthony walked and faced his own past and his own ghosts, I could help him keep going, too. Maybe the sky was big enough to swallow both of our pasts. Maybe it was big enough to absorb the pain and trauma of all the veterans who had ever lived. Those of us still living just needed to get out there. We couldn't fight each other's battles. But we could at least walk alongside each other. We could make each other feel a little less alone.

My solo pilgrimage was now a partnership. Anthony and I were able to put our heads together, use the creative energy and ideas that had been stifled at the nonprofit because of politics and red tape, and plan a mission the way we wanted to. We sprung into a frenzy of activity: Get a website up. Set up a Facebook page. Run to Mequon to meet with that potential donor. Find another rucksack that I can use since you're going to need yours now. Find sleeping bags, socks, a way to carry water. Let's pop over to Laacke & Joys to see if they'll sponsor us. Did you call that guy from Fox 6? Call him, he's a vet and was in the army reserve band. He can hook us up with media coverage in every city from here to Los Angeles. Beck got us booked on that talk show. We still need to decide where the trek will end — is it Santa Monica Pier, like we thought, or would the Los Angeles VA Center be better? Work with so-and-so to figure out what we're giving away to people who donate to our crowdfunding campaign. Make a video for the crowdfunding campaign. Call back that nonprofit that wants to donate water to us throughout the trek. Wait, are we calling it a *trek*? Yes, we're calling it *Veterans Trek*.

(By the way, Beck really thinks we should use an apostrophe in the *Veterans* part of *Veterans Trek*. She said it could be *Veteran's Trek* or *Veterans' Trek*, but there should definitely be an apostrophe in there somewhere. I don't know, man, you're the one with the English degree. I think you could read it like trekking is something veterans *do*, y'know? Veterans eat. Veterans sleep. Veterans trek. Okay, cool, no apostrophe.)

Donations poured in. Anthony and I raised money so we could still pay our bills while we were gone. We raised money to buy gear and food and supplies. We raised money for the nonprofit, where Anthony still worked with guys like Jack and Ken. We raised money to raise awareness around the issues veterans faced when they came home from war — things like addiction and homelessness, unemployment and anxiety, PTSD and not-just-PTSD, something else, something I couldn't quite put my finger on.

To our great surprise, fund-raising was the easiest part of preparing for the trek. The same people who never knew what to say when we came home from war finally had something to do — they'd just been waiting for us to give them the chance. It had never dawned on me that people had always been ready and willing to help but just didn't know how. Can you imagine a couple of military veterans asking people to donate their hard-earned money to help them heal the parts of themselves that couldn't be healed on their own? Can you imagine me, or Anthony, staring into a video camera and saying, "I'm all fucked up. I've tried everything to help myself, but nothing works. I don't know what to do. I need to heal. Please, help me do that."

Neither could we.

So we didn't do that. Instead, we made a video of Anthony sitting in a black leather easy chair in his living room as he read the children's book *Goodnight Moon*, by himself, with no children in sight. In the video he's thumbing through the little board book, with its stiff, paperboard pages, nodding his head introspectively and scratching his chin contemplatively, as if he's reading Confucius. You can see magazines and a glass of ice water on the end table next to his chair, books piled sloppily on bookshelves along the far wall in the background, his daughter's blanket tossed carelessly over the back of a dining room chair; the perfect picture of a man alone at home, unguarded.

Suddenly, Anthony looks up and stares right into the camera, startled.

"Oh!" says Anthony with a twinkle in his eye, "I didn't *see* you there!"

He then tells the viewer why we are doing the trek — to raise awareness of the issues impacting *all* veterans — issues like homelessness, addiction, and suicide. He says that in particular we are walking to raise money for the nonprofit so we can help local vets in Milwaukee and Madison, Wisconsin. Anthony doesn't mention the gnawing desperation for relief we both crave, the broken shards of souls we carry inside us, the utter sense of defeat and helplessness we'd both felt when faced with life after war. He doesn't mention those deeper, more personal reasons we are going on the trek, because he has to uphold the pact.

You didn't know there was a pact?

Sure, there is. I was sure of it, then. This unspoken, often unconscious pact between combat veterans and civilians has three parts.

First, veterans must be self-contained, self-sufficient, and selfless. We must live for others and put the needs of others above our own. While we're in the service, we put our fellow soldiers first and the needs of the group above our own. Once we're out of the service, the pact dictates that we remain *the ones who help*, not the ones who *ask* for help. Our vow when we join the military, whether we serve for a few years or for life, is to give and not receive.

Second, if I come back from war and something's wrong with me, the pact dictates that I work it out on my own, without civilian support or involvement or knowledge. If I'm not *man enough* to "suck up" the terror of war, if I need to seek professional help, if I need to become a person who asks for help instead of a person who helps others, I should keep it quiet. My silence allows the image of the selfless hero — the one who asks for nothing and needs nothing and lives to protect and serve, the one who can bear the trauma with dry eyes and a raised chin — to remain intact.

Third, hide all evidence of war. Hide it forever. Bury it deep.

We don't just go to war to preserve freedoms and the American way of life — we go to war so civilians don't have to. They don't have to go to war physically, and they don't have to go to war spiritually. We go so they never have to crawl into the belly of the beast and experience war from the inside. And if we really keep our promise, they never even have to *hear* about it. If we really serve and protect, we protect them from even having to think about what went on "over there." And we shield them from the war that rages within us when we come back. We do this most effectively by never talking about war. We do this most effectively by smiling and nodding and saying, "You're welcome" when a civilian says, "Thank you for your service."

Do people know, when they thank us for our service, that our service didn't just happen in the past? I imagine most people offer their thanks for the past, for the service that happened on deployment or during the time the veteran was an enlisted woman or man. But when you sign up to serve, you're serving for life. So any thank-you should be made in reference to the service being provided right then and there — the great protection being offered by the veteran who's choosing not to share his or her experiences of war.

They don't tell you that when you sign up, do they? They leave that part out of the sexy recruiting videos. Even if everything goes like it's supposed to in those videos — you train for war, you go to war, you love war, you love the adrenaline rush, maybe you even love to kill, it makes you feel like a man, it makes you feel patriotic, it makes you hot, you can feel the testosterone rushing through your veins — even if you find that you feel no shame for killing; even if you feel no shame for feeling no shame for killing, which is the least likely scenario of all these unlikely scenarios, you still have to lie about it forever.

You have to protect civilians from all that by lying — about what you saw and what you did, of course, but also about how you felt about it all. That's the most important lie of all. Your vow of protection isn't just to protect them from being blown up, or from the fear of being blown up. It's to protect them from the secret knowledge you're walking around with every day as you walk among them: that people are capable of the sickest acts imaginable. Sicker than the sickest acts imaginable. And sometimes the people who do the sick shit don't feel any shame for what they did. And sometimes, they even enjoy it. And in some cases, the only reason an individual is still alive, driving to work, having a baby, going out to dinner, is that the person at the table next to them did some sick shit, and did it for them, and found that they enjoyed doing it, and now has to sit at dinner knowing they're a monster, and now has to wonder how a monster can live among humans without destroying them, and now has to look at the individual they're protecting from the truth with the envy of all envies: the envy of their total and complete ignorance of it all.

With Veterans Trek, Anthony and I treaded dangerously close to breaking this pact. Our fund-raising campaign was an opportunity for people to finally fulfill the legitimate longing they had to ease our suffering. But it was also a threat to people who didn't want to know how the sausage was made. They knew, maybe subconsciously, that supporting us was buying our silence. They knew that without their help and support, everything that veterans kept locked deep down was going to come out. The homelessness, addiction, devastation, and suicide were going to emerge from behind the closed doors of apartments and homes and cars and schools. The twenty veteran suicides a day was going to jump to two hundred. And they wouldn't be able to ignore it anymore. And ignorance is bliss.

You know how certain people get irritated when they order an extra-hot-venti-one-pump-nonfat-six-scoops-of-matcha-absolutely-no-foam-green-tea-latte and it comes back slightly under 205 degrees? If veterans broke their unspoken pact of silence and started speaking up about war, those people wouldn't have the luxury of that irritation anymore. They'd know it didn't matter because they'd have found out about things that *do* matter. Once they learned how insurgents would kidnap entire families and give the man of the household a choice: watch your wife and children get murdered or become a suicide bomber, they'll never again enjoy the rich indulgence of ignorance. Once they learned the things that can't be unlearned, their coffee wouldn't taste the same, no matter what temperature it was.

The donations were our reward for honoring the pact and maintaining our silence. The donations were solicitations to continue to carry the burden of war on our own. The donations were pleas to never reveal the things we had seen. Please, take this money, go take care of yourselves, get all veterans to take care of themselves. We want you to heal. We need you to heal, so that you don't unravel, and in unraveling, drag us down with you.

Sixty-six people donated to our Indiegogo campaign to raise money for Veterans Trek. Most of them were veterans. Of those who weren't, only a few of them had ever asked Anthony or me anything about what we experienced during our time at war. They wanted to help. Without realizing it, they wanted us to not *need* their help. Deep down, they desperately wanted never to know.

One day, about a month into planning the trek, I called Ethan out of the blue.

"Tommy Voss!" said Ethan, surprised. His voice glowed warm in the thawing spring. "How's it going, man?"

"Just calling to check in," I said. "It's still cold as fuck, but it's getting warmer."

"Yeah? I'm outside right now — in shorts and a T-shirt," said Ethan. And for what had to be the eighteenth time, "You need to get your ass out to California, man. I keep telling ya!"

"About that," I said.

"Yeah?" asked Ethan.

I paused, not sure of how to say what I wanted to say.

"About coming out to California…well, okay," I said, finally.

"*Yeah?*"

"I'm coming out. But I'm gonna walk, so it's gonna take me a while to get there."

"No shit?" said Ethan.

"Yeah," I said. "It's turning into this whole thing. Like a trek. We're raising money and everything. Me and another OIF vet. People seem to be into it. We're not gonna take rides, either; it's really gonna be walking the whole way. Anyway, I'm trying to get some gear together. You got a ruck I can borrow?" I asked.

"Tommy Voss, I'll tell you what. Not only do I have a ruck you can borrow — I'm gonna mail it to you. I'll fucking mail it to you today."

"Thanks, man," I said.

"Don't get all excited," joked Ethan. "It's just a loan. It's my ruck and I want it back!"

"Understood," I said, smiling. "I'll walk it back out to you."

"Deal," said Ethan.

In the midst of all the help and support and the momentum of the trek, the suicide tape that had been running in my head for so long slowly began to change. I was so used to looking for a place to do it. A bridge. An overpass. A desolate stretch of highway. But with the trek to look forward to, with 2,700 miles of space and sky calling my name, Milwaukee's bridges and overpasses and highways began to morph in my mind's eye. They no longer looked like places to end my life. As spring turned to summer, they looked more and more like places of promise. I started to hope that the realm that existed where I wouldn't have to feel this way anymore existed here, on earth. That death wasn't the only option. That maybe I could feel better and stay alive at the same time.

15

SEEN

In summer 2012, a year before Veterans Trek began, Anthony had signed up for a study at the University of Wisconsin–Madison. As part of the study, he took a meditation workshop designed to help veterans heal from the trauma of war. He wanted me to take the course with him, but in order to get accepted, I'd have to go through a bunch of preliminary interviews first.

I was curious about meditation. When I was going to school at UW–Milwaukee after I got back from Iraq, I felt especially drawn to it. I didn't really think of meditation as a way to heal from war; it felt more like a hobby I might want to try, like taking Brazilian jujitsu classes or playing the ukulele. But any time I'd tried to learn more about meditation, it never really seemed to work out. Like when I went to sit with a Zen Buddhist monk at a meditation center in Milwaukee. I remember staring at a wall with my eyes half-open, trying to stay still when my ass hurt like hell. After the meditation was over, I asked if it was cool to move if I was in pain.

"Of *course* you can move," said the monk, irritated. That was all she said to me, and I left.

I knocked on the door of that same meditation center when their website said they'd be open, but no one came to the door. I called other meditation centers around town, but no one picked up the phone. I remember thinking, *Fuck it, then*, and giving up on meditation, even though I still felt pulled in that direction. Maybe it was the Eastern philosophy thing, or the mysticism thing, or the otherness of Buddhism, the trendiness of it then, the fact that it wasn't the Catholicism of my youth that gave meditation its allure. Maybe the floor of the meditation center wasn't as cold beneath my legs as the floor was during Mass as a child, when I'd sunk between the pews to play with trucks or color in coloring books as the priest droned on and on. Maybe the incense smelled better. Maybe the people at the meditation center, going through a different set of prayers, touching different-size beads, really believed in the prayers they were muttering. Maybe they felt the peace and lived the love they chanted about instead of mentally handing out demerits to families who didn't show up to church or who showed up but wearing the wrong clothes. But no one answered the door, and no one picked up the phone. So I gave up.

"What kinds of questions do they ask you in the interviews for the meditation course?" I asked Anthony.

"Man, they ask you everything," he said. "They ask what sort of violence you were engaged in during war, did you see people die, everything."

After my experiences with Jack, Dr. Campbell, and EMDR

therapy, I was done talking to people about my experiences in Iraq. Talking didn't work for me. Talking didn't undo the past. The last thing I wanted was to be the subject of a study with a bunch of grad students who'd make me talk a lot and nod at me with big, serious eyes and say "Hmm" for hours a day.

"Forget it," I said. "I'm not doing it."

But Anthony did it. He learned some special breathing exercises he could do to calm himself down when he felt anxious. He liked it. Like EMDR, meditation worked for him. Why wasn't I as susceptible to these treatments as other vets? Was I doing something wrong? Or was I just more broken than anyone else?

After Anthony finished the workshop, the meditation instructor brought a filmmaker, Michael Collins, to meet with him. Michael wanted to ask Anthony about his experience taking the meditation course. Michael was an Emmy-nominated director best known for *Give Up Tomorrow*, a documentary about a Filipino man, Paco Larranaga, who was wrongly accused of murder and sentenced to death. After the film came out, there was an uproar in the Philippines and around the world in support of Paco, with people everywhere calling for his release from prison. Because of the film and the support it generated on his behalf, Paco was ultimately taken off death row. Michael's next project would be focused on veteran reintegration after war, but he didn't yet have his star subjects.

Lots of independent filmmakers have to constantly raise money to produce their projects, and Michael was no different. He spent a lot of time on crowdfunding platforms like Indiegogo, both to fund-raise for his own films and to connect with other filmmakers and potential subjects for his films. One day, as he was watching videos online, Michael stumbled on the video Anthony and I had created to raise money for Veterans Trek. He saw the black leather easy chair, the magazines on the end table, the copy of *Goodnight Moon*. He saw the great, bearded man sitting in the chair, talking about helping veterans stay alive after they'd survived war.

"Hey!" he said. "I know that guy!"

He saw Anthony, the man who'd said, *Yes*, I liked the meditation course, and *yes*, meditation helped me a little bit.

Michael emailed Anthony. Remember me? he said. I'm working on this film about veterans. Then Anthony emailed me. And before I knew it, there was a film crew from New York setting up lights in my parents' living room, asking my mom what I was like as a kid and making off with dozens of home movies of me that were so old, they'd originally been shot on Beta.

16

TRAINING DAY

On the first day of training for Veterans Trek, Anthony puked all over the passenger-side door of his car. That day, it was flaming-black-walls-of-hell hot outside. Our goal for the day was to walk eight to ten miles — less than half our daily goal for the actual trek, when we hoped to knock out twenty miles a day. So ten miles should have been no big deal. Piece of cake. We chose the Eisenbahn State Trail because it was close to Anthony's house, and because it was as flat as a pancake — they'd removed a bunch of train tracks and paved over the paths with smooth, sparkling cement.

I don't remember who first set the pace, but it was too fast for us both. There we were, hustling through the heat like a couple of out-of-shape speed-walkers, backpacks filled with water bladders and thirty-pound rice sacks to add weight, huffing and puffing, both of us trying to keep up with the other. We couldn't have been more than four miles in when Anthony, his face beet-red with sunburn, stopped and threw his hands in the air.

"I'm done," he said. "I'm calling it."

Anthony stopped walking and crouched over with his hands on his knees, breathing heavily.

"Holy shit," he said, wiping sweat from his forehead. His giant feet had already broken out in giant blisters.

"We're so fucked," he said.

"How the hell are we gonna do twenty miles a *day*?" I groaned, doubled over next to him.

Anthony looked at me mournfully and shook his head. In that moment, we both realized that in addition to promoting the trek and doing interviews about the trek and posting on social media about the trek, we probably should have been training for the trek, too. And not just, like, two weeks before it started. It was too late to do anything about it now. We were completely committed, with no way of backing out. And we were completely out of shape and painfully unprepared — even to walk four miles, apparently.

When he finally caught his breath, Anthony tugged at a dry-ish patch of T-shirt, wrapped it around his sweaty hand, and used the makeshift mitten to pull his phone from his pocket. Then he called his wife, Holly, and asked her to come pick us up. A few minutes later, Holly's car appeared at the top of a steep hill overlooking the trail.

Anthony and I inched slowly up the hill, one step at a time, intermittently placing our hands down on the ground. We crawled upward like mountain-climbing babies, our calf muscles contracting as if we were giving birth to new legs.

No sooner had we escaped from the sun into the cool cavern of Holly's car than Anthony felt the full effects of the heat.

"I feel sick," said Anthony.

"Are you gonna puke?' asked Holly. "Should I wait or drive?"

"Just give me a minute," said Anthony.

Holly kept the car in park, and the three of us waited in the air-conditioning for Anthony's nausea to subside.

I knew it wasn't just the heat that was making Anthony sick. It was the stress. After months of planning, we thought we had everything in place for the trek. Especially the important things, like a way to access food and water throughout our journey. For food, we'd pack beef jerky and dehydrated fruit and carry as much as we could in our rucks. We'd then ration our remaining donation money to buy cheap gas-station food or whatever happened to be nearby when we stopped to camp for the night. For water, we'd partnered with a nonprofit organization called Friends of Water! They donated water and offered to have it shipped to various waypoints all along our route. Volunteers would go to the waypoints, pick up the water, and take it back to their houses. Then Anthony and I would meet with the volunteers, either at their houses or another point along our route, to get the water.

Earlier that summer, the founder of Friends of Water! assigned us our very own intern, whose sole job was to make sure our water would be ready and waiting at each waypoint along the journey.

Before the trek started, we called up to double-check on our water.

"Hey, guys!" chirped the intern — *our* intern — when we called.

"Are we all set? Will we have water at every waypoint from here to LA?"

There was a slight pause on the other end of the line.

"Yeah, so about *that*!" said the intern.

"Yeah?" we said.

"Do you guys think you can, like, reach out to someone at the rest of the waypoints to have water *delivered*?" asked the intern.

Anthony's eye widened. "Um, *no*," he said. "That's what *you've* had three months to do."

"Oh! So. Today's, like, my last day before I go back to school!" said the intern. "So..."

So we only had water through Iowa.

Meanwhile, more and more veterans were reaching out to us. Most were supportive. Some even asked to join us on the trek. But others were less than thrilled with what we were doing. I remember one particular troll who wrote us a message through our website. I can't remember verbatim what he wrote, but the gist was something like this:

Hey, Tom and Anthony, I'm a Vietnam veteran and I heard about what you're planning to do. Just know that if you make the mistake of following through on this trek, I WILL fly from New Jersey to Milwaukee to protest your walk, and I will NOT be alone. EXPECT IT!

The first day of Veterans Trek was during Harleyfest, when tens of thousands of Harley motorcycle riders descend on Milwaukee from all over the country. It was sort of hilarious to picture some wrinkled New Jersey vet shouting something menacing but inaudible into a lone megaphone, drowned out by the roar of the hogs. But I was shaken by his message.

In saying that I needed to heal the wounds of war, I seemed to be saying — whether or not I meant to — that all combat veterans needed to heal from the wounds of war. I was ready to acknowledge my trauma and face it head-on. Anthony was ready to walk beside me and face the darkest parts of himself. We didn't quite have the water thing figured out. And after our failed start at training, we didn't even have the *walking* part figured out. But we were ready to give our best effort at healing. At the very least, we were ready to try.

But what if others weren't ready to heal? What if, in finally facing my soul wound, I was turning away from everyone who wasn't ready yet? Was I turning my back on the veteran community if I committed to reclaiming myself?

As Holly slowly pulled away from the hilltop, Anthony's lunch — and our hopes for a quick and easy few weeks of training — splattered against the car door.

17

HERO'S SEND-OFF

I stepped onto the podium and adjusted the microphone. One hundred and fifty faces turned toward mine. Some people smiled. Some looked serious. Some fanned themselves with their event program. Some wept with the emotion of the moment — my parents, Beck, my Aunt Polly. They wept because I was there, standing in front of them, and alive. They wept because they remembered the Christmas when I was overseas in Iraq. They remembered that Christmas because it was the Christmas my mom baked a thousand cookies. One cookie for every car that drove by that year, its tires threatening to stop in front of our house, its driver threatening to be a notification officer in his Class A uniform, his shining boots marching along the winding path to our front door to destroy our family forever. They wept because my body came home, but the part of me they knew and loved never did. They wept — well, my mom wept — because Beck and I were both still single, and as she looked at all our family and friends gathered in one place, she said mournfully, "This is the closest I'll ever get to having a wedding."

And people wept because maybe now that lost part of me was going to finally come home from war — even if I'd have to leave first to go find it.

Anthony's family was there. So was Kimmy. She'd happened to be in town from Boston, where she lived and worked now. She sat in the back, away from those in my closest circle, wearing dark sunglasses and sitting straight and tall. Standing behind her was the mayor of Milwaukee, Tom Barrett; a reporter who'd called me the night before and was hoping for an interview; and the Milwaukee county executive, Chris Abele. Abele had donated $10,000 of his own money to the nonprofit where I'd worked (and where Anthony still worked) in support of Veterans Trek. He promised to donate another $10,000 to the nonprofit if Anthony and I made it to California. He was standing there in the heat, next to the mayor and all the most powerful people in the city, all of them in button-down shirts and suits and clothing not conducive to 90-degree temperatures, all of them waiting to hear the speech I hadn't prepared.

It was August 31, 2013, the inaugural day of Veterans Trek — the beginning of our walk across the country. The journey began at the Milwaukee County War Memorial, my hometown's monument to veterans of the past and present. Earlier that morning, hours before the event began, I sat in the shade of the memorial overhang, sweating through a cotton T-shirt and splitting my gaze between the blue lake and a bronzed statue of a soldier's boots. In the stillness of the heat, the empty chairs in front of the podium began to fill with ghosts. There was Sergeant Diaz and Sergeant Clark. There was my platoon-mate Luke, with his self-inflicted head wound, the bullet hole gaping. There was the ghost of my platoonmate Max, lounging in the spectral recliner where his family had found him. His ghost was wedged in between the empty chairs and was visible only to me. The four spirits stared at me expectantly, as if they were ready to follow me all the way to California.

"Check one, two, three. Microphone check, check, check."

There's something about a sound check that makes you realize you probably should have prepared a few words.

"What are you gonna say?" I'd asked Anthony.

He was trying to comfort his crying eighteen-month-old daughter, Madeline, who was sweaty and sticky like only an eighteen-month-old can be.

"I'm just gonna thank everyone for their support. Like, thank the people who've donated and helped make all this possible," said Anthony.

"Then what am *I* gonna say?" I asked.

Madeline wailed, and part of me wanted to wail with her. We'd been working for months to raise money and awareness for the walk, and people from all over the state and country had answered the call. Now that the day had finally arrived and we were being honored with a big send-off, I really wished I could be the hero everyone wanted me to be. Give the big speech. Smile for the cameras. The problem was that like a lot of veterans, I didn't feel like a hero. Not at all.

As people started taking their seats, Anthony and I stood to the right of the podium. A Vietnam veteran who'd found healing through Native American spiritualism had brought sage to smudge us. Wearing a trucker-style hat and some sort of tribal pendant around his neck, he lit a sage bundle and began waving it so the smoke wafted around our legs and backs and over our heads. I closed my eyes. The earthy, pungent smoke clung to my beard and clothes. The vet murmured a blessing so we'd be cleansed of the past and blessed along our journey. Maybe my Catholic family felt a little uncomfortable at this open display of non-Catholicism. Or maybe they saw the symmetry between the sage smoke and the incense burned during Mass. Maybe the heat of the smoke and the heat of the day would help to break the pain of the past like a fever, or sear it shut forever like a brand across our hearts.

Up on the podium, I faced the crowd and introduced myself. I wiped the sweat from my eyes. If only it were, like, seven degrees cooler. I tried out a few opening lines in my head: For those of you who don't know me, this is who I am. Or maybe, this is what's left of me. All the seats were taken, so the ghosts of Clark and Diaz stood next to me behind the podium. I felt sweat trickle down the back of my neck. Maybe it would help if I pretended it was 50 degrees instead of 150, which is what it felt like.

I opened my mouth, and words started to come out.

"Um, we're not just doing this for us," I began.

We weren't just doing this to reconcile the things we should have done with the things we actually did. We were doing this to remember the veterans without a voice. The veterans who were in their holes. The veterans who'd never be with us again.

As I talked, my vision shifted away and back, present to past, like a split-second intercut in a film. A cool breeze seemed to dry my skin. I could almost feel Clark and Diaz put their hands on my shoulders. Wait, did the blue sky just change color?

"We're doing this for those who were taken from us too soon," I managed.

My throat felt like it was closing in on itself.

"If we could just take a moment of silence."

The silence of reflection is also the silence of death. In the space of that endless silence, all I could think of was escaping. I had to start moving, or I felt like I'd be standing still forever, sucked into the silent realm where Clark and Diaz lingered. But our friends, family, and those we'd lost deserved a moment to remember and be remembered. They deserved the hero they wanted me to be. So I held that space for them. I looked down at the ground and focused on the cool relief of 50 degrees: Milwaukee in October. San Francisco in January. Mosul, Iraq, in the dead of winter.

A pair of bare feet kicked up dust in the street. They must have been calloused enough not to feel the broken glass beneath them. The feet began to run, scrambling over themselves toward our vehicle, moving with purpose, in earnest.

"Motherfucker," breathed Ethan, his weapon gleaming beneath a cool, gray sky.

We saw the same feet. We must have had the same thought.

Our vehicle splashed past that unholy spot where the waste of the neighborhood pooled in a steaming pile. I didn't notice the smell anymore.

Someone's radio crackled with instructions.

"Stop. Wait there. *Wait.*"

The vehicles ground to a halt — a direct invitation for attack. Ethan and I peered through the dust. The drainage of yesterday's dolma and the pair of feet were the only signs of life at 9:00 AM on a Monday morning in a city of 1.8 million. The presence of our brigade was enough to fill a ten-block radius with a silent symphony; it was the sound of civilians cowering in fear, civilians seething with resentment, civilians making love and bombs in secret bedrooms behind flimsy metal doors. Shutters were closed to keep shrapnel from slicing the necks of those who hid behind them. In this place, death was a promise kept more often than not.

The feet were attached to a child. He emerged from the dust and floated toward us like a ghost, moving closer and closer until Ethan let out a sigh of relief. He was too young. It would be at least another year or two before they'd recruit him to be an insurgent. Another year or two before the sight of him would cause us to drop into our vehicle, before he'd shoot at us first, before we'd shout, "Contact!" and return fire. But on that day, the only threat he posed was his insatiable, ravenous, near-murderous lust for candy.

I dove into the Stryker from the air-guard hatch above. In the darkened hull, I climbed over heavy boots and past dirt-caked uniforms, dodging backsplash from dip spit and the hot stream of piss pointed into an old water bottle. I pulled the latch that released the rear ramp. Outside, the lighters of privates flickered at the tips of stale Pine Lights cigarettes. The boy's feet carried him closer and closer to our vehicle like heat-seeking missiles.

"Cal!" I barked, whacking the hatch of Team 3's Stryker, which was stopped in front of ours. Our armored vehicles had eight wheels, two periscopes, a computer system, a pneumatic system, an engine system that could be replaced in two hours flat — and no air-conditioning. My radio crackled, and the vehicle hatch lowered slowly. The scent of sweat and dusty fatigues mixed with the shit-scented air. Cal shot me a look I knew by heart: Why the fuck were we stopped?

"Toss me that candy, Cal," I said.

I nodded to a crinkled package of what we liked to call "grandma candy." It was filled with cracked peppermint and Jordan almonds sent to us from overseas — the stale stuff nobody else wanted.

"Fuck you, Voss, that's mine!" grinned Cal. He thought I was asking for a piece of his chocolate bar, which he snatched protectively and held against his chest.

Cal was handsome and clean-cut, with an all-American, almost nostalgic quality about him. He looked as if he was fighting in World War II instead of Operation Iraqi Freedom. If it weren't for the wiseass smirk on his face, I'd have almost mistaken Cal's nineteen-year-old energy for wholesomeness. And if I wasn't so busy trying to stay alive, I might have noticed that he reminded me of my grandfather. Maybe that was what Bampa looked like when he was crawling behind enemy lines on Iwo Jima to take the hill from the Japanese — strong and self-assured. Confident in his mission against a clearly defined enemy. Scared as hell, sure, but able to overcome his fear because of his training, wipe out the Japanese position, conquer the hill, and live to see the end of the war — even after suffering a sucking chest wound and being placed on the beach next to a stack of dead bodies. Yeah, if I wasn't so distracted just trying to stay alive, I might have seen glimmers of Bampa in Cal's grin. It was the way you looked when you knew you were being of service. When you were sure of your purpose. When you knew, somehow, that you were becoming a hero. It was a look that couldn't survive for long on the face of a soldier fighting guerrilla warfare. Where the enemy hid in civilian clothing. Where you were never really sure who you were fighting or what you were fighting for.

"I don't want your chocolate, man," I said. "Gimme the grandma candy."

As I leaned into the rear compartment of the vehicle, I felt tiny fingers tugging on the camouflaged canvas of my uniform. Don't turn around. Don't make eye contact. *Don't make eye contact.* Cal hurled the bag at me. It was practically intercepted by the owner of the feet, but I snatched it midair and accidentally locked eyes with him. Big, brown orbs stared straight up at mine. He didn't smile or speak. His face was dirt streaked, and his hair was matted with mud. His filthy face annoyed me.

The silence in the street broke slowly. I heard a few more feet thudding on dirt as they sprinted toward the promise of unwrapped cellophane. Then the low murmur of "Mistah, mistah!" grew to "BOO-blay, BOO-blay," the desperate plea for rock-hard bubble gum. The crowd of children, who tended to parade behind our vehicles in ripped T-shirts and gray puffy coats, who tended to wear the same clothing no matter where we were in the city, who tended to whine and throw rocks at us and shout curse words nonsensically, stumbled into the street like clubgoers in the drunken dawn. The promise of root beer barrels and stale butterscotch was too tempting to resist, even under threat of a car bomb.

"Mistah! Mistah!"

"BOO-blay, BOO-blay, BOO-blay!"

I was the parade master. I swept fistfuls of grandma candy from my pack as best I could with my gloved hand. Pieces fell to the ground, and skinny fingers reached between my boots to snatch them. I sent up a shower of candy behind me, then fistful after fistful after fistful. The little one, the boy, was getting shut out by the others. He was too small and they were too fast. I wanted to help him. Don't get involved. *Don't get involved.* Don't look them in the eye. Don't make eye contact with the kids who could kill you a year from now. With the kids you might have to kill tomorrow.

I made the kids do the candy dance. With my weapon slung over my right shoulder, I moved my hips from side to side — up with the right, down with the left, then switch. You want candy? Dance for it. I've seen too many dead bodies this week. Dance for all the lives you're destined to take. Dance for your cousin, who just tried to blow us up. Dance so we can all pretend you're not about to be recruited to kill us.

"C'mon," I said. "Let's see it!"

One boy flailed his arms, imitating me. Another shimmied his hips as his friends looked on. Cal and I laughed at them dancing. A joyless laughter. Ethan watched from the hatch. Someone videotaped us dancing. We did this to entertain ourselves. Or maybe to feel like we could control something in a place that was out of control. Or maybe to punish and humiliate the children because we hated them for begging us for something more than candy, something we couldn't give them.

I threw the kids another fistful of candy as a reward for dancing. There was a moment, right after I'd thrown the candy into the air, when I could pretend I was the hero I thought I was supposed to be. It was the moment when the kids looked up at the sky. And when they looked up, instead of stray bullets and mortar fire, they saw something good washing down on them.

And our dance became a dance of joy and not of war. And for a split second, we forgot that all of us could be blown to bits at any time.

But that was just a moment — nothing more. The candy still fell to the ground. The children still begged. The reflection of the winter sky gleamed on the barrel of a machine gun that was pointed straight into the crowd of kids.

"You may put the candy into your pocket," we'd tell the kids.

"You may not take anything *out* of your pocket," we'd say. "No rocks, no weapons."

"If you throw rocks at us, you'll see inside the barrel of my M4," I'd say.

The kids knew it. And I knew it, too.

I'm not a hero.

In an instant I was back on the podium in the heat. The children, now shop owners or refugees or college graduates or dead, were back in Iraq where they belonged. The moment of silence was over.

"Thank you," I said to the crowd.

They applauded. Their eyes beamed. They were looking at me, but they must have been picturing someone like Bampa on that hill in Iwo Jima. They were smiling at their own ideas of a hero, passed down from generation to generation, idolized and idealized by the shifting, fluid, flattering nature of memory.

When the ceremony was over, just about everyone in the crowd stayed. They milled around as if Anthony and I had just tied the knot and they were waiting for the bar to open. They sat on chairs and stood in groups and waited for their turn to shake hands with the war heroes before we left.

Kimmy waited behind everyone else. I spotted her in the crowd out of the corner of my eye. Whoever I was shaking hands with got about 8 percent of my attention once I saw her standing there. She was waiting to talk to me, but she wasn't waiting for me anymore. In Boston she had a job. A life. A serious boyfriend who'd later become her husband, and then the father of their child. She'd have a son.

We embraced. I was a sweaty mess. I pulled her into my dampness, unembarrassed that I already stunk, because she knew my stink, because she knew me.

I peered through her sunglasses, searching for her blue eyes, looking for the life I could have had with her. But all I saw was the great, impenetrable distance between her and me. That distance didn't exist because of time. It was there because she got to stay innocent forever. She got to carry our sweet, youthful innocence into adulthood, where she'd set goals and meet them, save for vacations and go on them, carry on family traditions and pass them down to her children. Where she'd get a good night's sleep most nights of her life and drink a reasonable amount of wine when the occasion called for it, and never think much about death until it was time, at long last, to face her own. And she'd do it all with a lightness of spirit I'd known only with her.

Are you ready? Are you excited? How long will it take? This is Anthony, this is Kimmy, nice to meet you, thanks for coming. All the stupid things you say when you can't say what you want to say. All the longing and love and what-ifs and I'm sorrys beating at the backs of our eyes, straining to meet between us, fizzling in the heat. But I could tell by her smile that...no. I could tell that all that was left of what we had was the fondness of memory, a nostalgia for what could have been but never was.

Thirty minutes into nonstop handshaking and hugging with all the people that mattered most in our lives, Anthony and I were both dripping sweat. It was 100 degrees in the shade, our rucksacks weighed ninety pounds each, and we wanted nothing more than to get on the road, already. We were convinced that each hand we shook would be the last. Maybe that's why, for an entire hour before we started walking, we never took off our packs.

Our rucksacks were so ungodly heavy because we'd packed everything we could ever possibly need in any possible situation on the road. So I had winter clothes, military-style boots, a single-person tent with a military Gore-Tex shell, a GPS tracker, an entire first-aid kit, a camel back filled with twenty liters of water, and enough beef jerky to feed an entire platoon. Not to mention all the stuff in Anthony's bag. It was like we were trekking 2,700 miles across an alien planet, where we didn't expect to see another living soul the entire time. It never occurred to us that if we asked for help on the road — an extra pair of socks, a beef jerky refill — it might have been gladly given. We'd already asked enough of our family and friends just by going on this trek. We'd already broken protocol as veterans by asking for help at all. Once we left Milwaukee, we were on our own. The burden of war was ours to bear. So we'd bear it by ourselves, across the country, never asking those we swore to defend to help lessen the load we carried.

18

COMFORT

When I first got home from Iraq, I stayed at my parents' house because I had nowhere else to go. It was a two-bedroom, midcentury ranch that was small but cozy — their effort at downsizing after my sister went off to school, I went off to the army, and the big white house we'd moved to during high school felt big and empty without us. The upstairs was decorated in my mom's signature style. It was country chic: homey maximalism with lots of burgundy and hardwood and oil paintings and baskets. The house was almost always so clean you could eat off the floor. The kitchen was filled with sunflower dishes and bluebird figurines; the dining room, with china and pink crystal we only used on Thanksgiving and Christmas. Above the fireplace was an assortment that changed with the seasons — a cornucopia of waxy fake flowers in the fall, my mom's collection of wood-carved Santa Claus figurines at Christmastime, tiny glass rabbits and pastel eggs at Easter. The objects were cleaned, dusted, and displayed with such reverence because they were reflections of the family, of its heart. A barren, modern, minimalist decor reflected a family that was cold and impersonal. But a hearth overflowing with decorations, a shelf bursting with trinkets and treasures, meant the hearts of that family were bursting with love.

On the first floor was my parents' bedroom and a den they used as an office. There was a third bedroom in the basement, but it didn't count as a bedroom because it didn't have a window. Since there was no window to the outside world, my dad decided to make the room itself a window into the past. He'd filled it with paintings and photographs and memorabilia of our relatives and ancestors. There was a hand-drawn family tree he'd researched himself and sketched in pencil. There were marketing materials from Bampa's many campaigns to become district court judge — "Voss" or "Voss for Judge" on signs and bumper stickers and posters. There were photographs of Bampa meeting with Bob Hope, Bampa sitting at a typewriter surrounded by my dad and his siblings when they were kids, Bampa's nameplate from his office at court, which read "Circuit Court, Branch 2, Clair Voss." There was a photograph of Bampa's Marquette University football team from the 1940s. In it Bampa stood tall and proud, with the subtle smirk of youth and eyes that had not yet known war. There was a slotted frame that had been filled with three carefully chosen photographs: Bampa in his marine uniform, Grandpa Bob in his navy uniform, and me in my army uniform. Beyond these there were dozens of other framed photographs of relatives living and dead; our family at a summertime festival in the early 1980s; baby me in an umbrella stroller wearing a blue bonnet; my sister in a striped sundress and curls holding an ice-cream cone and glaring at the camera. Many of the pictures were so old they were faded and yellowed and of people we'd never heard of or people we had asked about once and forgotten. Some great-great-great-great-someone-or-other from the 1800s who looked scarily like my dad or eerily like my sister.

Beck and I had both stayed in that room off and on, throughout our twenties and into our thirties. It was the place you stayed when you came home on break or leave. It was where you camped when you had to come home because you were broke, or your big plans hadn't worked out, or the relationship ended, or you decided to finally move back to Milwaukee, again, for good. We called it the room of ghosts, where we were watched over by the eyes on the wall while we slept. It made coming home a reminder of where I came from. It made me remember where I fit in the lineage of our family. The photographs were meant to remind me that I was part of this family, that I belonged there. That I was a servant among servants. But after war, all I saw when I went into that room were the faces of people condemning me. Or worse, the face of someone who might have understood — someone who'd discovered how to heal the soul wound inside them — but who was gone forever.

When I got out of the army, my mom and dad set up the room of ghosts for me so I'd have a place to sleep. They fitted the pull-out couch with fresh sheets and warm blankets and soft pillows. My first night back, I told them good night and went down to the room to go to sleep. I looked at the made-up bed for a long time. I wasn't used to having nice things. I wasn't used to having a home-cooked meal. I wasn't used to sleeping with fancy pillows and soft comforters. I knew then, as I looked at the perfectly made bed beneath the pictures on the wall, that my mom and dad would never understand what I had experienced, that all they could do was offer a warm meal and a soft bed, that they believed and hoped that a warm meal and a soft bed would be enough; that if I felt and saw warm, safe things back home, those things might neutralize the dangers that lingered in my mind. They had no idea how hopeless it was to hope to heal, even a little bit, from the right pillows. Had they sent me to sleep on the basement floor, I would've felt better. At least they'd have met me where I was; at least I would've felt they understood, at least a little, how hard and cold I'd become.

Then I looked at the pictures on the wall. The military heroes, the servants and martyrs, the ancestors I'd never met, the people who'd given me life. The people whose lineage I was supposed to be carrying on. I looked at the pictures of my Bampa accepting medals, signing important papers, standing next to his beautiful wife, Betty, at some important public event. I wondered if it was hard for Bampa to let other people take care of him after the war. He was so severely wounded at Iwo Jima that he didn't have a choice — it took six months of rehabilitation at naval hospitals in Guam, Honolulu, San Francisco, and Chicago before he could walk again. I wondered if he felt like a hero. I wondered if he would've understood why I couldn't sleep in a safe, warm bed. Did he feel, when he came home from war, that he didn't belong in the family anymore? I doubted it. He must have felt, along with everyone else, that he'd fought in a war worth fighting. Whatever trauma he carried was a necessary burden he took on in order to defeat a clear enemy and achieve a clear goal. Even Bampa wouldn't have understood what it was to fight without knowing what you were fighting for; to fight for your survival in that moment, to sacrifice lives, just to survive. Even if Bampa would have understood, he was like all the others I had lost — nothing more than a memory. A picture on the wall.

I left the bed made, stepped outside the room of ghosts, and laid down on the basement floor at the bottom of the steps. It was cold and hard and what I knew. It was comfortable to me. In the early morning, when my dad came downstairs to feed his fish, he tripped over me in the dark.

19
UNLOAD

Our goal for the first day of Veterans Trek was to walk twenty miles. Anthony and I headed west along Wisconsin Avenue as the film crew followed us in Anthony's jeep. Jerry, the producer, drove; Melissa, the director of photography, filmed out of the back of the moving jeep; and Michael, the director, hopped on and off like he was riding a tourist bus. There was lots of excited shouting as we moved away from the war memorial and lumbered down the sidewalk with our rucksacks on our backs.

"Why don't we hop in the jeep and forget this whole thing?" asked Anthony.

The volunteers laughed. Two of them walked alongside us for the first few miles. Beyond the financial donations and donated gear and offers to house us on the road, there were dozens and dozens of people who wanted to walk with us. Most asked to walk for a few miles, or an afternoon, or a whole day. But many of them asked to walk with us the whole way. Anthony and I welcomed the day players, but we said no to anyone hoping to join us for the whole trek. We wanted awareness of veterans' issues to grow, but we wanted to keep the actual trek confined to just us two, at least for most of the time. There were insurance and liability issues to consider. But more important, aside from the film crew and the news crews, the mayor and the county executive, the talk shows and interviews and Facebook fans, we still hoped to find the time we both craved to be alone and face the past. We couldn't do that without the support of our community. But we also couldn't do that surrounded by a pack of other vets or volunteers 24/7.

Just five blocks in, we ducked into a fire station to change our shirts. The white cotton was too thick in the heat, so we switched to more breathable nylon. The firefighters gave us ice water and let us cool off in their garage. Up the road at Marquette High School, an all-boys private school and Anthony's alma mater, three hundred boys lined the sidewalk to high-five us as we passed.

We were just 4.2 miles from the war memorial when I felt the first hot spot start to pop on my heel. If you were supposed to be walking twenty miles today, and if today was supposed to be followed by 135 consecutive days of walking twenty miles, and if 150 people, plus thousands of online supporters, plus the clinging ghosts of dead sergeants, plus Veterans Everywhere were all counting on you to *walk the damn twenty miles*, a blister — even the *tiniest* blister — is a big, fat problem.

"Anthony," I said.

"Yeah."

"I'm getting a blister on my heel."

"*Really*," he said.

At the Wisconsin Humane Society, 4.7 miles from the war memorial, we stopped again. (If you're keeping track, we'd only moved another... half... mile.) A supporter was waiting for us with a cooler of frozen towels. We stood in the shade, and he wrapped the icy cloths around our necks like we were in a barbershop.

Just a few blocks later, Anthony stopped walking altogether.

"I need to sit down," he said. "I feel like I'm gonna puke."

We sat on the side of Bluemound Road. Anthony dry-heaved beneath a tree while I tended to what had become multiple blisters. Michael was in heaven — what makes for better footage than complete failure right out of the gate? The camera crew captured our sorry state on film. Five miles down. Only 2,695 miles to go.

That night we sat, bewildered, swollen, and sore, in a cool garage that belonged to Anthony's friend. We'd only made it 10.1 miles — just half our goal for the day. We'd stopped a block south of my parents' house in Wauwatosa, tempted by bottled water and air-conditioning. We'd failed, and we'd run home to Mommy and Daddy, which somehow made it even worse. Not wanting to burden my parents, Anthony and I got picked up by a friend who lived in Waukesha. We'd decided to take rides to and from supporters' homes if they volunteered to put us up for the night. The same with accepting rides to events and interviews. Rides were allowed, as long as we got a ride back to where we'd stopped walking and kept walking from the exact point we'd left off. Anthony asked his buddy for a box. We emptied our rucksacks of all but the most necessary supplies. Goodbye, winter jacket. So long, snow pants. Why the hell did we think we'd need walking poles, anyway? Pound after pound after pound, the weight of our burden was slowly lifted. We didn't need the extra baggage. We had to trust that what we could carry was what we needed to survive. And that the rest would be provided to us somehow.

When we were done, the box was full and our bags were thirty pounds lighter. Instead of carrying this weight all by ourselves, we were going to have to trust that we'd be given what we needed, when we needed it. Even if the not-just-PTSD-trauma-thing made it hard to feel the goodness in ourselves, we had to trust that goodness still existed in others. And that it would be enough.

20

LOCKED AND LOADED

Seven days and ninety miles into the walk, I was sitting on a park bench on a trail in the Wisconsin countryside, staring at a wasp that had just landed on my foot. Anthony and I were stopped on the trail west of Madison so I could change my socks. When you're walking twenty miles a day, your feet become these precious infants that you have to swaddle and change and coo to constantly. But I hadn't been protective enough, allowing my feet to be exposed to the hot sun and fresh air long enough to be infiltrated; the sticklike feet of the wasp poked right into the tender, wet flesh of a freshly popped blister.

For the past week, Anthony and I had been getting our asses kicked across the great state of Wisconsin. We were finally alone — Michael and the film crew had flown back to New York after the send-off in Milwaukee. They'd fly out again once we got closer to the Iowa border. From there, they'd meet us at set points along our route: west across Iowa and Nebraska into Colorado, until the uncompromising ridge of the Rockies forced us south through the Raton Pass into New Mexico. Route 66, which ran from Chicago to Los Angeles, was one of the first highways in the US highway system. Its official end point was on Santa Monica Pier in Los Angeles. We'd follow old Route 66 whenever we could, passing into Arizona and finally crossing California to the sea. But for now, there was nothing to do but put one foot in front of the other in the August heat.

In the far western suburbs of Milwaukee, past Carroll University in Waukesha, we picked up the Glacial Drumlin State Trail. It was a truffle of a trail, all smooth, crushed limestone, the kind of trail that's meant for bicycles and slim runners in cushy sneakers. At first our feet practically wept with glee, but as the day wore on we became exhausted again, and hungry, and thirsty, and I suddenly had to take a dump — bad. We rounded a bend and saw the white-and-green pickup truck of a Waukesha County Parks employee. She was driving slowly, as if she'd been looking for us. She pulled to a stop and smiled widely, her long, brown hair pulled back in a neat ponytail that hung over the collar of her freshly pressed uniform.

"Hey," I said, "do you know where the next rest area is?"

"You're in luck!" she beamed, fanning her arm out the truck window and pointing down the trail like a flight attendant performing a safety check.

"There's a restaurant just a few turns down the trail, about a mile away. Take a right, then a left, then a right, and you'll be there in a jiff!"

"Thanks!" I said, mentally calculating if I'd be able to make it a whole mile to the toilet.

The park employee smiled, and I swear to God a gleam of sunlight twinkled off her teeth like in a toothpaste commercial. When I looked back, her truck was gone.

A mile down the trail, after a right and a left and another right, the restaurant was nowhere to be found. Four miles down the trail, when I had seriously considered taking a shit in public in broad daylight in plain view of the runners and cyclists, we finally found the place. Far from the mecca of rest-stop restaurants the park employee had implied, it was a dump attached to a gas station. I made it to the toilet just in time, but not without mentally cursing the park employee and her stupid sense of direction and her complete inability to gauge distances, and wasn't that, like, her *job* as a park employee — to know where stuff was in the park?

By the time we made it to Madison, we both had blisters the size of golf balls all over our feet. During a TV interview with a Madison news station, Anthony asked the reporter if she wanted to see his blisters. Before she could answer, his socks were off and he was waving the glistening flesh for her and all of Madison to see.

"If you're going to show this during dinnertime news, make sure to have a warning on the screen," said Anthony.

The reporter frowned and wrinkled her nose. We limped on.

Anthony was leaning over me with his jaw hanging open. I'd sat down to change my socks on the Military Ridge State Trail, a gravel trail that stretched west from Madison and wove through forty miles of green farming valleys. If you've never seen wasps up close, they look a lot like bees but skinnier and meaner-looking. Their stingers poke out of their butts like tiny, venomous tails. Bees' stingers only come out when they're ready to sting. But wasp stingers are locked and loaded at all times. My blister had popped completely open, leaving a bridge of skin that bubbled across the side of my foot to my heel. It was so big that there was, in fact, an *entrance* and an *exit* to what had been my blister. As I stared down, horrified, the wasp began to crawl inside my blister. First it had to fold its wings back so it could fit inside. Then it started going in headfirst. All six of its legs were moving. I could feel them prickling me, like someone was playing a tiny piano inside my skin. It wasn't like it was going through a tunnel, either — I could feel this pulling sensation, this tension where the wasp pressed against the skin from the inside. The fucker was *burrowing* through my blister. Getting right up in there. I didn't know if I should smash it and risk it stinging me, or not smash it and risk it stinging me.

"What do I do?" I asked Anthony.

"I have no idea, man," said Anthony.

So we waited, and watched, to see what would happen. I could see the dark shadow of the wasp, it's black-and-yellow body inside my skin, as if through translucent glass. When the head emerged, its stinger was still sticking out the other opening of the blister, and its body was covered by my skin. A full thirty unbelievable seconds later, the wasp wriggled its body out the blister's exit and flew away.

21

CHEESE COUNTRY

Hot, blistered, and miserable but happily unstung, Anthony and I continued west across Wisconsin to the aptly named Cheese Country Trail. It's a shortcut we'd picked because it would dump us straight into the town of Darlington, where Anthony's grandparents lived, and where, I imagined, we'd spend a cool, relaxing night sipping homemade lemonade and noshing on his grandma's home cooking. Even better, Anthony's grandpa told us that there was a ton of shade on the trail, which would be a welcome break from the sweltering sun in our faces. All we had to do was make it a few more miles.

At the trailhead, we stumbled over baseball-size rocks that had been laid in piles between large boulders. Even the shoulder of the trail was filled with rocks and boulders hidden beneath tall grass. Twenty minutes later, it dawned on us that the boulders and rocks weren't simply marking the trailhead. The boulders and rocks were what made up the trail — because it was an ATV trail. A smooth ride with tons of shade if, and only if, you were going 45 mph on a motorized vehicle. If only we'd hung on to those walking poles. Dehydrated, blistered, and brutalized by the sun, I looked over at Anthony. He had clenched his hands into fists and was making a jerking motion to pull them apart in the universal human sign for "pull the plug." We each picked a boulder and sat down, wet with sweat and defeated.

Suddenly, the low rumble of an engine started closing in. Minutes later, Anthony's cousin drove up on his ATV. He was bright-eyed and grinning at us, his stocky frame guiding the vehicle to a stop, like a cowboy slowing a steed. Anthony and I just sat there, sweating.

"Just coming to check on you guys!" he said, cheerfully. "Just coming to see if there's anything you need!"

"We need to go back in time to talk ourselves out of doing this walk in the first place," Anthony said.

"But the ENTIRE FAMILY is waiting for you at the end of the trail!" said the cousin. "C'mon — it's only six miles away!"

He waited for us to groan our aching bodies back upright. Satisfied we wouldn't sit back down again, he climbed back onto his vehicle and started the engine.

"I almost forgot!" he said. "We thought you could use this."

He handed Anthony a four-foot branch that someone had removed from a tree for use as a makeshift walking pole. Anthony took it like a reluctant Moses who'd just been told he had to part the Red Sea, when all he really wanted to do was take a nap.

It took us four hours to walk six miles. Anthony's feet got so blistered that he couldn't put his full weight on them and had to rely more and more on the walking stick. We must have looked like a couple of ninety-year-old men making their way across an obstacle course. An hour after his cousin drove away, Anthony even had a blister on his *hand* from gripping the walking stick so hard. The sun set, and we stumbled over rocks in the dark, cursing the day we ever decided to do this stupid walk.

As I climbed over rock after rock, each step a punishment, I realized we *couldn't* quit. We had to move through the pain, because there was no other way to get where we were going, and we couldn't let Anthony's family down. In that moment of pure, painful misery, the love of those who loved us was enough to keep us going. Even when we had nothing left to give, their love for us carried us down the path. It breathed our next painful breath. It led us six more excruciating miles to Anthony's grandparents' house — a house his grandfather built with his bare hands.

We reached the house in the dark. I'd never been so happy to see a house in my life. It was decorated with garlands of fake fall leaves and an Oompa Loompa scarecrow with a white, ruffled clown collar. Inside, hanging crystals over the kitchen sink — shell, starfish, dolphin — foretold of the cool, tranquil night's sleep ahead. The embroidery hanging on the wall promised that this was "Home Sweet Home."

As we unloaded our gear, my body started to register the temperature in the house, which felt pretty damn close to the sweltering temperature outside. Anthony's grandpa could put up with the Halloween decorations in August, the silverware displayed lovingly in a wooden case hung on the wall, the blue floral wallpaper that wrapped around the periphery of the living room. But what he couldn't abide by, what he couldn't stand, was the idea of bastardizing the house he'd built with modern indulgences. Indulgences like, say, air-conditioning. He did allow for the odd fan or two. There was even one on the second floor, where we slept. It was built into the woodwork in the hallway outside our rooms, which were both filled with collections of antique china dolls dressed, just like the scarecrow, in white lace clown collars.

After being stuffed to the brim with homemade cheeseburgers and french fries, we climbed the stairs to our steamy den.

"Grandpa," called Anthony, "can you turn on the fan?"

Grandpa had called Anthony a "softy" for getting a blister on his hand from the walking stick, but he indulged us now. The fan whirred on and I could feel all the hot air being sucked out of the second floor. He must have had a stopwatch, because I swear Grandpa left that fan on for no more than three minutes on the dot. He shut it down, and the heat from outside wrapped its sweaty tendrils around us once more. That night, I got four hours of sweltering sleep. But somehow — maybe because they believed in us — the next morning, we kept going.

"I highly recommend you don't do this," the police officer said.

He narrowed his eyes and frowned.

We were finally at the Wisconsin-Iowa border, where a huge black bridge arched over the Mississippi River. It was a two-lane bridge that was meant only for cars. There was no sidewalk or shoulder for pedestrians to walk on, which was why this off-duty cop had pulled over in his personal vehicle and asked us what the hell we thought we were doing. It didn't help matters that there was a film crew in front of us crammed into a minivan, its back hatch wide open and flapping in the breeze so the director of photography for that day's shoot,

Gabriel, could get the shot he wanted. The movie crew was back on the trail. They'd planned intermittent stops throughout the walk; they'd fly from New York to wherever we happened to be, stay for a few days to film, then fly back. It seemed like they'd planned their stops based on where we'd be walking — somewhere interesting, or beautiful, or in this case, dangerous.

We limped along slowly — Anthony's entire left foot was one giant blister — with the film crew in front of us and the cop crawling along slowly behind us. When we were just a few feet from the end of the bridge, I looked back to see a wide-load semi barreling down the road. There was no room for us and the truck on this bridge — its load jutted into the oncoming traffic lane without apology. If we didn't haul ass, the truck was going to whip us off the bridge into the river below.

"Let's go!" I cried, willing my limbs forward faster than my body wanted to go. We cleared the bridge just as the truck roared past, honking loudly as it went.

Anthony and I glared at Michael and the crew, who were cheering the awesome shot they just got for the film.

That better make it into the final cut, I thought. (It did.)

We'd walked less than two hundred miles and had more than two thousand to go. Everything in me wanted to quit. No wonder some veterans spend their whole lives denying their trauma. If we don't admit it's there, we don't have to heal it. And we don't want to heal it, because healing it hurts — especially in the beginning. The first steps away from pain are always the most painful.

22

UNBROKEN

Rick Lisowsky was lying on the floor with a gun to his head when his wife walked in and found him. She got there before he pulled the trigger. After that day, his promises not to end his life were half-hearted. Suicide was a constant threat in the Lisowsky home, no matter how much Rick loved his wife, no matter how beautiful their two young children were. Life after war was simply too much to bear, because for Rick, the war never ended.

A combat veteran like Anthony and me, Rick was on permanent disability because of the many health problems he had from his time in the service. In Iraq he'd been exposed to burning chemicals and toxins released in the air from giant burn pits, which the army used as huge, open-air incinerators. Burn pits were enormous, flaming piles of trash. The military used them to get rid of medical waste, leftover food, ammunition, petroleum, plastic, rubber, chemicals, aluminum cans, metal scrap, and human feces. Rick was also "blown up" a lot during his time in Iraq, meaning he was in or near explosions when they happened. The doctors and his family thought that his medical complications could be because of his body's response to the shock waves from all those blasts. In Monument, Colorado, Rick was more than seven thousand miles away from the burn pits and bomb blasts in Iraq, but his body couldn't seem to forget them. His cells were enslaved by the black, billowing smoke, the smoldering tires, the plastic bottles that curled into themselves and became the air he breathed, the potent booms of the car bombs.

After serving his country for eight years, Rick now spent most days lying in bed. Rick couldn't stay hydrated on his own, no matter how much he drank. He had to have a permanent IV placed in the artery under his collarbone and had to take weekly hydration shots. Rick no longer defecated into a toilet; he had a colostomy bag attached to a stoma in his small intestine to collect waste.

According to the VA, symptoms like Rick's offered "inadequate or insufficient evidence" that certain health problems were due to burn-pit exposure or other service-related trauma. The VA said symptoms related to burn pits were temporary. They said once you stepped away from the burn pits, your symptoms would subside. They said there was no verifiable reason why someone like Rick would be having the symptoms he was having.* The implication of the VA's stance, as far as I could tell, was that problems like Rick's couldn't possibly be caused by time spent in combat.

---

* Public Health, "Studies on Possible Health Effects of Burn Pits," US Department of Veterans Affairs, May 16, 2019, https://www.publichealth.va.gov/exposures/burnpits/health-effects-studies.asp.

In spite of the depression he must have felt, typical of so many combat veterans and compounded tenfold because of his failing health, Rick Lisowsky reached out through the darkness. He found Veterans Trek on Facebook. He joined the four thousand others who followed us, many of them veterans or family of veterans, all of them fast on the draw with an encouraging comment or emoticon when we posted updates on the walk. If we were in or near their city, our supporters were even faster with an offer to stay in their guest room, crash on their couch, camp in their yard, or stay in a hotel they'd paid for.

Rick saw how Adam and Patti and Jackie and Ron and Patrick and Jason and Sarah and Sim and Rob and Tyler and Matt and Ryan and Aaron and Bill and Linda and Sharon and Braxton and Deb and Mike and Eric and another Mike and Jim and Carri and Alain had offered us a place to stay. He saw how people chased us down, tracked our path on a GPS, invited us to their Veterans Day celebrations, asked us to speak to their Boy Scout troops, walked miles upon miles with us in the heat and rain and snow, and drove to slow stops alongside the road to bring us buckets of chicken to eat while we walked. Sure, a sandwich might have been more practical, but beggars can't be choosers.

Anthony and I had made it across Iowa and into Nebraska in a flurry of activity: get our miles in — twenty a day, ten to twelve on a light day. Stay on schedule. Keep raising money for the nonprofit back home. Manage the awareness campaign to promote the trek on social media and get the word out through local news stations. Coordinate drop points for water and gear. Meet with other veterans and listen to their stories. We were busy, our bodies broken down at the end of each day, our minds consumed with the pressure to keep going, make a difference, make an impact for the greater good, for veterans everywhere.

What about the healing part? I wondered often. *Is this it?* I knew I needed to take action, so I'd put one foot in front of the other. But then what? How do you actually heal yourself? What do you actually *do?* I wasn't sure, so I just kept moving and looking up at the sky, hoping for something to happen.

In Iowa we'd met a marine-turned-rancher-turned-pastor who told us that life demands a response. You can respond to trauma by curling in on yourself like a wilting plant, or you can respond by taking action to face the pain and move through it. That sounded good, but I *was* taking action. What's walking twenty miles a day if not taking action?

Next, we met a pastor dressed like Abraham Lincoln. He told us he was drawn to Old Abe because Lincoln "just never gave up." Anthony asked him for his favorite Abe Lincoln quote. He didn't know any. Then he told us that 50 percent of pregnancies end in abortion and that the Ultimate Fighting Championship was the downfall of Western civilization.

Then we met a waitress at a Pizza Ranch in Independence, Iowa. In the restaurant Anthony and I made a beeline for the same table — the one with the best view of the entrance. After being in Iraq, neither of us could sit with our backs to the door. Not anywhere. When entering a public place, we noted every entrance and exit so we'd be the first to notice a gunman and the first to get people to safety. Once you've been trained to think this way, you can't turn it off. Not even in a town of six thousand people, where the main points of interest are an agricultural history museum and a nineteenth-century mill. With eyes on the door, we could almost relax and enjoy our meal.

We could even laugh when we noticed we were in *Independence*, Iowa, and our check total for the pizza buffet came to $*17.76*. When we pointed out the coincidence to our waitress, she stared at us blankly.

"1776?" said Anthony. "And this is Independence?"

She shook her head, confused.

"America gained *independence* from England in *1776*," said Anthony.

"I didn't really pay much attention in school," said the waitress.

For every strange stranger we met on the road, we met even more people who felt like family. My certainty of the pact that existed between veterans and civilians became a little less certain. Not everyone was trying to buy our silence. Some people really wanted us to finish the walk. They wanted the issues we raised to become part of the public consciousness. They thought the conversations we were having about the issues impacting veterans should be taking place on a national level. A surprising number of them wanted to hear about our time in the service. They asked questions. They listened to the answers. They asked more questions. They took us out for chili and cinnamon rolls. They told us that chili and cinnamon rolls is, in fact, a thing.

It was easier to accept help when we were taking action. Walking twenty miles a day in all sorts of weather with heavy packs on our backs for a cause bigger than ourselves made us feel worthier of help. Like we'd done something to earn it. We offered our steps in exchange for hot water and baked chicken. It was easier to accept help from other veterans, too. They knew just how hard it was for us to ask. We knew just how important it was for them to be the ones helping.

As it grew colder and winter grew near, we were more motivated to ask for help from our supporters a bit more directly, and with more urgency. It had taken us four long, painstaking weeks to make it across Nebraska, which meant we'd be entering Colorado during the second week of November, when the average temperature at night hovered just above twenty degrees. We had to haul ass and make it out of the mountains before the snows came.

Sometimes we'd ask for help on Facebook. Other times, Anthony would make a humble plea on the blog he'd been keeping. He posted diligently, whenever we stayed somewhere with Wi-Fi. It was a way to track what happened on our travels and keep our tribe updated on our progress, pit stops, and pitfalls. But blogging was also a way for Anthony to work out the things he'd gone on the road to work out: what it meant to be a good husband and a good father, what it meant to be a good person once you had seen and done bad things, what it meant to reach out to others and ask for help when things got hard instead of hiding in the basement.

"If you live in or are familiar with people in these areas," Anthony wrote, "it would be much appreciated if you'd email us and inquire on our route to see if we're going in the direction of those you know. See if those people would be willing to shelter us for an evening or two, depending on the circumstances.

"In the beginning and to date," he continued, "we have been extraordinarily blessed by the number of people who have invited us into their homes, paid for a room for us, fed us, and made certain we were okay. Hopefully, we didn't use all that up."

We hadn't. Rick Lisowsky wanted to help us, too. Once we reached the great wall of the Rockies, we could no longer walk west. Instead, we'd head south along I-25, trying to make it to

the Raton Pass to New Mexico before winter hit. Rick lived
about fifty miles south of Denver and right along our route.
But with a wife and two little kids and his hydration port, Rick's
place wasn't ideal for a couple of backpackers and all their gear.
So Rick's mom, Deb, said we could stay with her.

Once Anthony and I made it past Arapahoe, Nebraska, and
walked from Cambridge to McCook; after we'd had dinner with
Boy Scouts in Benkelman and crossed the state line into Fort
Morgan, Colorado; after we'd worked on a ranch in Wiggins
and stayed with a veteran for five days in Denver, we headed
south to Monument. There we stayed with Deb for most nights
between November 23 and December 2. We spent Thanksgiving 2013 with their family. During the day, we'd get our miles
in, then get shuttled back to Deb's. In the evenings, Rick would
come to have dinner with us and talk to us about his time in the
service, his deployments in Iraq, his body's ongoing rebellion.

Rick wrote on our blog, "[The trek] is important to me because I have been down and felt like there was no hope and just
wanted it to end. That is a dangerous place to be. I am tired of
our brothers and sisters feeling the same and seeing the only
way out as suicide."

One night, around Deb's kitchen table, Rick told us he
wanted to walk with us the next day. At first we wanted to say
no. Rick hadn't been doing much physical activity because he
got dehydrated so easily. Plus, it had already started to snow.
Anthony and I were worried. Deb was worried. But Rick was
determined.

"I had to show myself that I can overcome this and that I'm
not broken," he later wrote.

He wasn't broken. Rick couldn't walk with us for a full

twenty-mile day. But he was determined to walk. So Anthony and I kept pace with him, only doing as much as he could do. I figured it'd be a mile, maybe two, before Rick had to rest, or stop for the day altogether. I was wrong. He wasn't broken. That day, Rick walked with us, in the snow, for twelve miles.

About the day he walked with us, Rick wrote, "They kept checking on me and motivating me, and I just kept pushing myself to make it with them. Because they have gone a lot farther than me, and I can at least try to make it for them and for our brothers and sisters that need these issues out in the public. If you get the chance to walk with them or host them, please take the opportunity. They are two awesome guys doing something great, not just for themselves but for all of us."

It had been easier to focus on other veterans and the greater good than to talk about the personal, more hidden reasons I'd wanted to walk in the first place. But maybe the two weren't mutually exclusive. I'd been looking for teachers and someone to point me in the direction of healing. And there was Rick, with his broken body, willing himself down the road and succeeding. There was Rick, proving his own strength to himself in order to give hope to others. There was Rick, worse off in many ways than I'd ever been. What more could I ask for in a teacher? What was I expecting to find out there on the road, some kind of medicine man or something? If someone like Rick Lisowsky could peel himself out of bed to walk, if he could find a place of inner strength when every cell in his body was weak, if he could offer to help us while accepting help from others, then I had no excuse. If Rick was willing to pull himself up like that, it was a slap in the face to him, and to all vets, if I didn't do the same.

23

WALKING WITH WOLVES

Anthony and I leaned into the hill as we climbed a dirt footpath that wove through heavy forest and underbrush. We'd been shuttled by the film crew into the foothills of the Rockies just outside Colorado Springs. All I could hear was the sound of my breath, my boots on the earth, and chirping birds heralding the late-afternoon light. I pressed into the steep incline, my legs tingling from the twelve miles we'd already walked that day with Rick, who'd gone home to rest and recover.

The path curved sharply. As we rounded the bend, Anthony and I came face-to-face with a man standing in the middle of the trail. He stared at us in silence. A wolf pelt adorned his head and shoulders. His face was painted black and white: black on top, like a Zorro mask that reached beneath his nose, and white on the bottom, where the paint disappeared beneath the top of his black-boned necklace. A stark, straight line cut across his face where the colors met halfway. Attached to the wolf head were three black-and-white feathers, which floated above his left ear, bobbing in the mountain breeze. Over his black shirt he wore a decorative panel made of dozens of white animal bones. A wolf medallion hung between the two rows of bones. His pants were fringed, and his feet were wrapped in moccasins. He looked at me, then at Anthony. He turned on his heel and continued up the path. Without a word to him or to each other, we followed him.

Just outside Pike's Peak, the highest mountain in that part of the Rockies, there's a town called Manitou Springs. It's there that a sudden burst of red rock pops against the gray, snow-capped background of the fourteen-thousand-foot summit. It was there that we followed the man with the painted face into the Garden of the Gods. At the end of the path was a canyon with two ancient-looking red rock formations that stretched toward the sky, then toward each other until they touched. You could see the place they'd melted into each other under the pressure of some ancient glacier long ago. The connected rocks formed a circular opening like a portal into another world. The layers of rock shone in the late-afternoon light in rich reds and rusts and pale pinks.

The man's name was WolfWalker, a Native American healer who'd come to speak with us as part of the film. I was agog. Was this guy for real, like a legit spiritual teacher, or was Michael just hoping for some dramatic cinematography? Together with his producer, Jerry, and his directors of photography — Melissa or Gabriel, depending on the location — Michael would find these epic shots and interesting people for Anthony and me to meet. Sometimes we'd hear cool stories or get some decent advice, like with the pastor who told us to take action. Other times all we had to show for these off-the-beaten-path photo ops were blisters on our feet.

WolfWalker jingled and tinkled with every step, the music of his clothing mixing with voices from above. There were tourists standing on top of the rock formations as we climbed into the garden. They milled around up there, snapping photos of the scenery with their phones and peering down at us curiously. They watched as WolfWalker lit the end of a sage bundle and used an eagle feather to fan the pungent smoke throughout the cavern to purify the space and bless us and the moment.

WolfWalker then maneuvered to a bench-like rock that was flattened and smooth as if it were man-made. His movements were slow and steady. The rock beneath his bench jutted out at the perfect angle for a footrest. He sat like he had been there before. Anthony and I laid blankets on the red stone where it sloped downward at a sharp angle. It felt like we were in the audience at an old, natural amphitheater and WolfWalker was the Greek chorus. He sat in silence. We waited for him to speak.

In the silence, I started to notice how richly colored the rock formations were. It looked as if they'd been painted in bold, appetizing contrast to the blue sky that opened endlessly above. I thought about how the dome of the sky curved over the gray, snow-capped mountains and the red rocks alike — even though the red rocks were completely out of place in this part of the range. Even though the red rocks weren't really supposed to be there. But for some reason that no one could explain, they were. After the flat, monotonous plains of the Midwest, where we were dusted by harvester trucks along empty highways, our search for answers crushed beneath an impersonator's top hat or the glazed eyes of a pizza buffet worker, after struggling through the snow with a man who'd had everything taken from him but his inner strength, we'd finally earned a moment of beauty.

"I have had many friends who have served in the military," said WolfWalker finally.

"My father was in the air force. One of my good friends, he was a sniper."

WolfWalker was surprisingly soft-spoken, with a thin, reedy voice that belied his size and strength. He told us that in some Native American traditions, warriors were received from the battlefield as heroes. Their return was momentous: whether they had won or lost the battle, their contribution was honored by the entire community. And whether they had won or lost the battle, they knew why they were fighting. If a period of healing or reflection was needed, the warrior was given time and space to examine his wounds. Only then, after taking the time for both spiritual and physical recovery, was the warrior expected to reenter society as a contributing member. But today's warriors often don't know what they're fighting for. Even worse, we return from battle without any kind of systematic reintegration process — not from the military, not from our families, and not from the larger community. And so the burden falls on us to make sense of the nonsense of war — the war we've just fought and the war that continues to rage within once we come home.

WolfWalker told us how his friend the sniper had been shooting at insurgents out of the back of a moving vehicle on the freeway. His bullet passed through the insurgents' vehicle and struck and killed a nine-year-old boy in the car behind them.

"That was something that always weighed very heavy on him," said WolfWalker. "I know you have your stories. If you could think of one thing that still haunts you to this day, and sticks with you, the one thing you carry deep with you.... If you could share that with me now."

He waited for Anthony and me to answer. Something about the question made me stare at the red rock beneath my feet. There was a flicker, and then a flash: my hiking boots became combat boots. From the ankles down, I was in a place where you needed military-grade boots in order to walk on top of the jagged rocks that made up the ground.

I could hear Anthony's voice. He was telling WolfWalker about an injured civilian he'd wanted to help but had left on the side of the road. He was saying that he had followed orders. That he was not supposed to stop to help the man. But that still, it had been him who had left the man there to die. He could have refused to follow orders. He could have stopped and helped. But he didn't. He did nothing. He'll never know what happened to that man.

Then it was my turn to share a memory.

It doesn't look like him, I thought. How could it, with all those tubes coming out of his mouth and the silver-dollar-size hole in the side of his head. Sergeant Diaz was laid out on a surgery table in the Combat Support Hospital (CSH) or "cash." Bandage wrappers and rubber gloves were strewn across the rocky ground. He'd been in there for no more than three minutes before the medics had emerged from behind the tent flap and told us we could come in and see him. We entered in pairs like animals in the ark, bracing for the flood.

It had been minutes before, on our way back to base, that we'd decided to get blown up on purpose. As I was riding in a Stryker, an improvised explosive device (IED) flashed on the screen of our digital map. The same alert was sent to every vehicle in the convoy. IEDs were usually made of old mortar rounds or artillery rounds that were packed with C-4. They'd be shoved into the trunk of a car, with a cell phone attached to the explosives. Someone might be blocks away, up on a building looking down, waiting for us to pass in front of the car where the IED was hidden. As soon as we got close enough, they'd call the phone that was attached to the IED, and BOOM.

On a typical day there could be dozens of IEDs planted throughout the city. We had Explosive Ordinance Disposal (EOD) teams who would blow them up safely, but they were so overworked that they'd usually have to just alert everyone to where the bomb was hidden, then go back to explode it when they had time.

That day we knew an IED was in our path and still active. If we had to, we could drive through it, trusting that our vehicles could take the hit.

"Hey guys, what's the call?" Sergeant Diaz's voice crackled through the radio.

I couldn't see my team leader because he was riding in another vehicle, but his voice made it easy to picture him. He was always riding the wave of his last joke or gearing up for the next punch line — you could just hear it. To amuse himself, he'd grown these big, nasty sideburns and a huge, dirty mustache that made him look like 1970s Super Mario. The facial hair fell within army regulations — but just by a hair. Something about the mustache made our friends in the Iraqi National Guard assume he was Iraqi, too. When they came up to us and asked our interpreter if Diaz was Iraqi, Diaz would beam. He'd nod like he understood them until it finally became clear that he didn't, and then everyone would have a good laugh.

"Route Buick is code black right now," said Sergeant Richardson over the radio. "Let's go straight instead and take the hit."

It was the safest call, really. That way we wouldn't leave a live bomb unexploded. Besides, we'd probably just have to change a few tires once it detonated, and then we could get back to base so Diaz could comb his 'stache.

Our convoy of Strykers moved forward slowly down the city street, the vehicles separated by minutes of space between them. The street was empty, the front of each shop sealed shut behind a sliding metal door. If we hadn't spotted the IED on-screen, the empty street and closed doors would have been a telltale sign something was about to blow up. Civilians would sometimes see the person planting the bomb and close up their shops and homes, bracing for the blast. Other times, news of the forthcoming bomb would be whispered between neighbors, like a cryptic game of Telephone.

As we approached the IED, the air guards took cover. The IED exploded. The blast hit like a kick in the chest. It sounded like those loud, booming fireworks that go off near the finale on the Fourth of July. Not the sparkly streamers or the squiggly snakes. The colorless ones. The phantoms. The invisible thunderclaps that should burst in the sky and cause a rush of fear and delight but instead explode ten feet away from you and render you deaf immediately. It's a few seconds before you start to hear ringing in your ears and feel your feet beneath your body. But sometimes that's a few seconds too late.

The air guards popped back up above the hatch to their positions, exposing themselves to the air like open nerves. Out of nowhere, automatic gunfire showered down from the rooftops. We fired back, but the faceless enemy behind invisible AK-47s was gone. Like always, we were hunted, ambushed, but never engaged. It's the warfare of men both economical and lazy: the least amount of effort for the most amount of destruction. They'd disappear as suddenly as they'd appeared, leaving us breathless and impotent in the dust. Wondering when and where they'd strike next.

The radio crackled again.

"Diaz's been shot in the head!"

My heart stopped. No one spoke. You were never supposed to name names or specify the type of injury over the radio. You were just supposed to say you had a casualty, which meant that someone had been injured. This, in order to prevent complete panic for those in other vehicles who can't see what you're seeing, who don't know if you're going to make it back to base in time to save him, who don't know if you're going to get ambushed again.

It must have been five minutes, but it felt like five hours before our vehicles finally roared past the gate of our base. When we blew past a checkpoint, the guy guarding it ran after our vehicles, screaming his head off. I must have exited the vehicle, because the next thing I remember was seeing Diaz's body crumpled in on itself. One guy held him under the arms, another under his knees. And then more of them, emerging from the vehicle. They were all covered in his blood. And one guy, he was up to his knees in it; the line of blood began at his knees like the line of paint on WolfWalker's face and was soaked all the way down to his boots, as if he'd been wading in blood. The guys kept coming out of the vehicle, in slow motion, like a clown car in a horror movie. And then all of us were there, pacing on the rocks, our boots kicking at the rough stone, waiting outside the cash.

A medic peeled back the flap of the tent of the cash. Twenty pairs of eyes looked at his.

"You can come say goodbye now."

I went in the tent and just looked at him for a little bit. I didn't linger. They had opened up his airway. Gotten the tubes in. Tried helping him breathe, but it was too late.

Outside my boots hit the stone, and then I felt my knees on the ground. I must have been crying because the rocks around my knees were wet. My old roommate was suddenly next to me, breathless from parking the Strykers and running back to the cash.

"Is he gonna be okay?" he gasped.

I blinked back tears and looked at him.

"No," I said.

We were paralyzed together on the rocks. Some guys talked, and some guys wept, and some guys felt nothing at all. An officer and a chaplain stood among us like hall monitors in case anyone wanted a pass to talk about their feelings. As if you could articulate loss and its meaning as instantly as the loss had occurred. We felt him, Diaz, as his light extinguished to nothing, and in that moment we all became nothing. We all became nothing but the hard rocks beneath our boots. And I remember, when I looked up from the wet patch of stone surrounding my knees, seeing guys lying prostrate on the rocky ground like they were the ones who'd been shot in the head instead of him. And no one yelled at me for taking my helmet off or told us to get our shit and get out of there, like they normally did if we were just standing around. And their silence was how I knew that this thing had, in fact, happened.

WolfWalker tried to pull me back into the beauty, but one boot stayed on the ground outside Diaz's tent. It was my turn to tell him about the thing that haunted me most.

"I can see perfectly...those moments. You know. When you're...seeing someone who's there one moment, and the next, you're seeing your buddies carrying him out of a vehicle."

And that was all I said.

WolfWalker said if you take the things that happen to you and try to push them down — if you try to keep the soft, muddy bottom of the pond undistributed — you never learn the lessons you're meant to learn from those painful experiences. Pain gets transformed to power when you stop running from it. When you finally realize you can't drink it away, smoke it away, medicate it, or ignore it. It will still be there, waiting for you to acknowledge it. Waiting for you to learn the lessons you're meant to learn. And so your only hope is to face it. To walk through it. To fully and completely accept it. Only then can the thing that hurts the most be the thing that sets you free.

But nobody can transform your pain for you, he said. He said in his tradition, nobody external could heal you. You had to take responsibility for your own healing. It had to come from you.

"You have to grab that power and say, 'I choose to learn from this. I choose to get my power from this.'"

WolfWalker said that we were now in a place where we could choose to learn from what happened to us during combat. We could choose to turn pain into power, turn it inside out, in a way, and use the broken parts of ourselves to heal ourselves instead.

"But it's work," he said. "It's a whole new way of thinking. It's being vulnerable. No walls. And it's being aware of everything around us. Being present to that. The great mystery of everything that surrounds us. And knowing that you are part of that."

Suddenly I understood why the talk therapy and the medication and the EMDR hadn't worked for me. It was because I hadn't been taking responsibility for my own healing. And because I hadn't taken responsibility, I hadn't been able to really accept the help I needed. When I first met with Jack, I did it because Beck had set up the appointment. When I first went to the VA, I did it because Jack said I should. When I did EMDR, it was because it had worked for Anthony. I was asking for help, but I wasn't able to accept the help being offered because I wasn't taking responsibility for the outcome. I put all the responsibility onto the person offering the help. I didn't have any skin in the game. If I wasn't willing to take responsibility, no wonder asking for help didn't help. When the treatment didn't work, I just blamed the person who'd treated me, threw my hands up, and walked away.

WolfWalker was saying that other people could point me in the right direction, but I had to do the work myself. If I asked for help, it was up to me to accept that help and make it actionable for my life. And if it didn't work, it was me — not my sister, not my social worker, not my psychiatrist, not society — who had to try something else until it did.

WolfWalker stood up. He walked slowly, deliberately, to the place where the two rock formations touched. Anthony and I followed him through the opening. He led us out of the canyon and onto a wide ledge that opened to panoramic views of snow-dusted mountain peaks beneath a blue, cloud-streaked sky. We had no idea such a beautiful view had been there all along, just a few feet from where we were sitting. Michael rolled the camera. Anthony told Michael that sometimes all it takes is a few steps in a different direction to give you an entirely new perspective on your life.

For a moment, Sergeant Diaz released his hold on me, and I stood with both feet firmly planted on red rock, leaning into the sky. I breathed in the beauty all around us. The clouds, the trees, the leaves, the rocks, the water. I looked up at the people standing on top of the rock formations, high above my head. WolfWalker said the beauty wasn't just all around us but within us, too. He said I wasn't separate from all that. He said I was a part of it. For a moment — maybe just a flash — I felt it, too.

24

DEER KEN

Michael wanted us to stop walking and sit still for four whole days. Anthony and I were finally in good enough shape to walk twenty miles a day with ease. We'd been hustling south from Monument toward Colorado Springs, moving as fast as we could to stay ahead of the impending winter. Frost clung to the needles of towering pines and peaks, which made us feel small in a way that felt big. The breath we saw in the air wasn't sour from alcohol but fresh enough to merge with the mountain air, which sort of made us feel like we were becoming one with nature. Which sort of made me feel like I was underneath the deck behind the blue house, rubbing smooth stones on the side of my cheek, back before it occurred to me that boys shouldn't cry. We'd met WolfWalker, who asked questions that begged answers. We'd finally learned to accept the kindness of strangers, our trained, ingrained mistrust giving way to acceptance of the help that poured across our Facebook page.

During our time with Deb and Rick, we'd finally felt like part of a community. We learned how to give and receive help so naturally, it felt like breathing. We were finally getting somewhere, or at least standing on the precipice of somewhere, and now Michael wanted us to stop.

And that's why, on a Tuesday morning in late November, we weren't walking but standing still in front of a stranger's front door — me, Anthony, Rick Lisowsky, Michael, and Gabriel. Above the door was a plaque that read Jai Gurudev. The plaque was attached to a two-story house in a forested neighborhood near Deb's place in Monument, where the houses were built into the foothills of the mountains. Our punishment for all this progress was four days of sitting around doing absolutely nothing — for *eight hours a day*. Michael had asked if we were interested in taking a meditation workshop from a teacher he knew. And because we wanted to help Michael out with his film, we said sure. Okay, maybe it was less like *sure* and more like *fine*.

One thousand one hundred and fifty miles in, I was in full-on mission mode. Eyes on the prize. Mind on the horizon. Always thinking about what's next. What's next. What's *next*. I had to process my life. I had to keep *processing*. That's what I was *doing*, I told myself, with each step I took. Besides, there were all those people out there rooting for us. Watching our progress. Cheering us on. This meditation course was not a part of the plan. We were on a mission, and every second we deviated from it felt like we were letting someone down. Not to mention the fact that winter could roll down like an avalanche at any second, and we needed to get out of the mountains as soon as possible.

Anthony had meditated before, in that workshop he took in Madison. Michael was an experienced meditator and had taken many meditation courses and gone on many silence retreats. He practiced a daily ritual of meditation and breath work, even when he was busy filming. I was still kind of curious about meditation, especially since it seemed to make Michael super chill and really present, even when he was under extreme stress. I just didn't want to take four whole days out of our trek to try it. Couldn't we just do a thirty-minute crash course and get back on the road?

The door opened, and there stood Ken, the teacher of the course. Ken was a thin, middle-aged man with a lean face, upturned eyebrows, and a smile that peeked out from under a thick, bushy mustache. In the short time it took for Ken to usher us inside and lead us downstairs, I was bowled over by his energy. Ken was so gentle, so peaceful, so intentionally calm that he made WolfWalker's peaceful nature seem rough by comparison. Twenty years of sitting still and breathing in and out had made this guy a human pond; he didn't speak so much as *ripple*. He waded in and out of interactions like some beautiful bird landing on the water. He gave off this powerful sense of acceptance just by standing there, listening to me talk. What I'm trying to say is that it was impossible to imagine Ken ever getting angry about anything. He was like Mr. Rogers, if Mr. Rogers had spent two decades in a cave somewhere just taking off his sneakers and putting them back on.

For hours upon hours, for four days straight, we sat in Ken's sunken basement, breathing in and out. The house was built into a hill, so what appeared to be two stories in the front was actually three stories in the back. The basement had these big picture windows that looked out onto this frosted backyard.

Beyond the backyard, the foothills of the mountains began their ascent. Tall pines trumpeted up the hills, heralding the towering peaks above. Back on earth, three combat veterans, a cameraman, and a film director sat cross-legged in front of their meditation teacher.

In between all the breathing and sitting and wishing we were back on the road, we listened to Ken share stories about the power of meditation. One time he was meditating on a tree stump in the middle of the Sierra Nevada mountains in California. (You know, like you do.) After about twenty minutes of meditating, he opened his eyes and saw that he was face-to-face with a deer — it was just a few feet away from him, standing absolutely still and staring right at him. Ken figured he was so calm that the deer no longer found him a threat. He thought that animals were naturally attracted to the inner stillness and peaceful energy people give off when they meditate. He thought that, at least for a moment, he'd somehow become one with nature. I flashed back to the wasp trying to become one with my blister. I was pretty sure my energy then had been anything but peaceful.

"Jai gurudev," said Ken.

There was that phrase again, the one that was on the plaque above his front door. Later I'd learn that it meant "Victory to the big mind." The idea is that there's this big mind, like a universal mind. Like maybe God or nature or something like that. It's like this one universal energy that permeates everything. You. Deer in the forest. A leaf on a tree. Everything. I think the big mind was what WolfWalker was talking about when he said we were connected to everything around us. Then there's the small mind. The thing you use to order coffee or do a math problem or wish you were famous or watch mind-movies of the deaths of your sergeants on repeat. The small mind makes you feel separate. The big mind makes you feel connected. The small mind is like a wave in the ocean. The big mind is the ocean itself. Anyway, when Ken saw the deer, it was like his small mind went and crawled under a rock, and his big mind took over. Ken and the deer became part of the big mind that connected them both. In that moment, they became one. And since they were one, the deer wasn't afraid to get so close to Ken he could almost have reached out and touched it.

Ken said meditation wasn't just good for helping you feel connected. It could actually transform the past. It could transform the pain of past trauma into power. (Wait a second, didn't WolfWalker say something like that?) Ken said that meditation was a tool you could use to actually *do* that — transform pain and trauma into healing power. And he was making it seem like it wasn't just guys like him who could do that; *we* could do that, too. All we had to do was let go of what happened in the past, if only for a moment. Stop thinking about what's going to happen in the future, if only for a moment. Instead, look within. Right now.

I tried to look within. I tried hard to stay in the present moment instead of thinking about the past or future. But as we sat there on that first day of the course, I found my mind drifting back to the road. I pictured myself walking with the ghosts of Clark and Diaz, trying to outrun them, maybe lose them in the mountains or leave them behind in the forest. When I did manage to stay focused on the present moment, I started to think about Anthony and Rick sitting beside me. Then I started to think about all the bad stuff we had in our individual pasts. I thought about the weight of what I carried inside. Then I multiplied it by three to account for whatever Anthony and Rick were holding on to. I pictured all our individual traumas pooled together in the air between our bodies as we sat there with our eyes closed, meditating. The memories formed this thick black cloud of trauma that polluted Ken's basement like vaporous tar. We may as well have all taken a soul-dump on his carpet or smeared spiritual bile across the sparkling glass of the panoramic windows.

If only he knew what he'd invited into his home, I thought.

This was never going to work. Did Ken really think that holding a finger to one nostril while breathing out the other could stop the bleeding in Clark's neck or patch the hole in Diaz's head? He must not understand. I participated. For the film. For Michael. But in my mind, I placed the bodies of Clark and Diaz on the floor at Ken's feet. I let their blood sink into his plush carpeting. I used their bodies to make a bridge between Ken and me, where neither of us would ever cross. This meditation stuff might work for normal people who are trying to overcome normal amounts of stress. But it wouldn't work for me because breath couldn't soak up blood.

Everyone's gonna think this was fake, I thought. *No one's ever gonna believe this.*

It was four days later, and we had about an hour left to go in the course. I still hadn't shaken the ghosts. I hadn't conjured my own inner Mr. Rogers. But maybe, for a moment here and there, there was a small experience of peace. A few flashes of silence breaking up the audio constantly playing in my head. A space on the floor in front of me where — for a split second — the ghosts of Clark and Diaz disappeared and there were no bodies. Just carpet. Just the basement and windows, Ken and his mustache, the guys, and me. It felt far away, almost imperceptible, but at one point I almost sensed a single ray of sunlight streaming into a dark cave, a sliver of hope for healing. That's how it seemed, anyway, until our final meditation.

We were sitting in the basement like usual, legs crossed, eyes closed. Ken was sitting in front of us, facing us, back straight in a chair. Beyond him were the glass panes of his picture windows, and beyond those lay the great, forested slopes of the foothills. Ken led us through a final breathing exercise. Then he told us to open our eyes.

Two deer were standing outside the windows with their snouts pressed to the glass. They sniffed the glass, then they looked at us and just stood there. Gabriel leapt toward his camera and pointed it at the deer. Rick's jaw dropped in wonder. Ken turned around to see what we were gawking at. He turned back to us with a small smile, like he was pleased but not surprised. Someone joked that Michael must have been out there, corralling the deer like a cowboy, tempting them with carrots or apples or something to get a great shot for the film. But Michael was sitting right next to us, shaking his head and smiling.

Holy shit, I thought.

"I wonder if I could use meditation energy to lure deer during hunting season," said Anthony.

The two deer nosed the windows and eventually sauntered back toward the forest, rejoining the small herd that had gathered in Ken's backyard. Maybe it was a trick; maybe Ken had spent years domesticating those wild deer to come when he blew a silent deer whistle that he'd hidden under his chair. Maybe it was just a freaky, freaky coincidence. Or maybe there was something to this whole meditation thing after all.

25

TAKEN FOR A RIDE

My eyes were still closed when I heard a sharp scraping sound. It was Anthony throwing open the hotel room curtains.

"Fuuuuuuck," he said.

My eyes popped open. Buckets and buckets of snow were coming down, except not quite. The wind was so strong, the snow wasn't coming *down* so much as being blown sideways. I could barely make out the hotel parking lot. The Rockies, normally visible in the distance from our room in Pueblo, had disappeared completely.

Anthony turned and looked at me. I looked at the snow. Then I hopped out of bed and started layering on all my clothes.

"Let's walk to the gas station," I said. "We'll pick up some food and come up with a game plan." I put on long underwear, a long-sleeved shirt, another sweatshirt, a rain jacket, and a winter hat. As soon as we stepped outside, the cold cut through all those layers like a knife. The wind whipped snow into small drifts on the sidewalk. American flags stood at attention, pulled taut from their poles as if frozen stiff. The wind had to be blowing at least 30 mph. Anthony and I pressed against the glass door of the gas station entrance with all our might. The door gave way, and warm air rushed to melt the tiny icicles that had formed on our beards during the ninety-second walk outside.

"Winter is here," I gasped, breathing hard between the hot dog warmer and the Slushie machine.

"We're pretty much fucked," heaved Anthony.

I couldn't disagree. It was 0 degrees outside, but with the snow and whipping winds, it felt like 30 below.

Back in the hotel room, we stood with our coats and hats on, holding our breakfast in wet plastic bags. Anthony looked out the window again and shook his head. Hadn't it just been weeks, or even *days*, earlier that we'd walked in short-sleeved T-shirts? Hadn't we pushed ourselves south as fast as our feet would go, galloping ahead of the imminent Colorado winter, sure we'd win the race? Wasn't Pueblo, less than a hundred miles from the Raton Pass to New Mexico, supposed to have one of the mildest climates in Colorado?

We checked the forecast for the next few days. Then the next week. Then the next few weeks. There was no change in sight: snow followed by snow followed by ice and more snow. Zero degrees during the day, even colder at night. It would be weeks before the storm subsided, but even then there was no guarantee of warmer temps.

We didn't have weeks to wait. Our very limited funds had been carefully budgeted to scrape us across the California finish line in five months' time — no more. Anthony had a job and a family to get back to. I couldn't afford to hole up in Pueblo indefinitely. How would we eat? Where would we stay? We didn't know anyone there. We didn't even know anyone who *knew* anyone there. Plus, we'd made a commitment to our donors and supporters to finish Veterans Trek in five months. If we paused or stopped, we'd be letting everyone down. If we paused or stopped, we might not get some of the donations promised us, like the $10,000 Chris Abele had pledged to the nonprofit when we finished. When we finished *on time*. If we paused or stopped, I was afraid we'd quit altogether. No. We had to keep moving. But we couldn't keep moving in *this*.

"I'm calling it," said Anthony, reading my mind. "We can't walk in this."

Technically, we *could* walk in a o-degree blizzard during the day. It would suck, but we wouldn't die. But we couldn't camp in a o-degree blizzard overnight. It would suck, and we *could* die. No matter how cold it was, walking all day made us sweat. Our clothes got damp and cold. South of Pueblo, the towns grew farther and farther apart — there were sometimes forty miles between rest stops. For at least the next week, we'd have to camp every night. There was nowhere to dry our wet clothes; if we hung them or laid them out in our tent, they'd just freeze, so our only choice would be to sleep in them. Crawling into a sleeping bag in negative temperatures in cold, wet clothes was suicide. And for the first time in years, I actually didn't want to die by suicide. In fact, I was pretty sure I wanted to live.

In the military we'd been trained not to care whether we lived or died. That's how you gauged your success as a soldier in combat — you knew you were doing it right if you didn't think twice about putting yourself in the line of fire to save someone else's life. You couldn't go out on missions and get blown up every day if you were worried about dying. You'd be paralyzed with fear and unable to do your job. In war the only way to survive was to give up any hope of survival.

In Pueblo there were no lives to protect but our own. There was no one to save but each other. But we'd been taught that our lives were most valuable when sacrificed. And we clung to that, even when there was no one around to die for. See, if you survived the bombs and shrapnel, you could physically remove yourself from war. What was harder was removing the war from yourself. A decade later, these imprints of war made death less scary than life.

So it was not out of the question for Anthony and me to knowingly and willingly put our lives at risk, to sleep outside in negative temperatures, to bravely choose death without fear. Because that, after all, was what we'd been trained to do. And that was the great lesson we'd learned in the army: our lives mattered most when we lost them. We mattered most in death.

Did we still believe that, all these years and miles later? There was only one way to find out. All I had to do was utter the five words that kept repeating over and over in my head. Five words to finally die a hero's death in Pueblo, Colorado, Home of Heroes.

We have to keep going.

We have to keep going, no matter what happens to us. *We have to keep going*, because we said we would. *We have to keep going*, because what we *said* matters more than being dead. *We have to keep going*, because just think of the headlines!

"Iraq War Vets Freeze to Death on Cross-Country Walk for Veterans' Rights"

"War Heroes Die Fighting for Veterans Everywhere"

"War Heroes Perish in Pueblo, Home of Heroes!"

I stripped off my soaking-wet clothes in the bathroom and caught a glimpse of myself in the mirror. My hair was matted and damp from my hat. My beard was wet with thawing ice and snow. I hadn't shaved since we left Milwaukee. Besides the promise never to take a ride, Anthony and I had promised we wouldn't shave until we reached the sea. My beard spiraled out from my chin in course auburn coils. It grew in a different shade than the hair on my head, as if it belonged to someone else entirely. It was as if two distinct, parallel paths were forming, and I had to decide which one to take.

I turned on the tap and splashed warm water on my face and beard, washing away the clumps of cold. I looked into my own eyes again. I spat the five words into the sink. A new phrase started to take their place. Six words this time.

I walked into the room and looked out the window. I looked at the wet layers of Anthony's clothing strewn across the hotel bed. I looked at Anthony, who was sitting on the bed, staring at the floor. I couldn't let us die in the mountains. I couldn't let the 1,049 miles we'd walked be a soon-forgotten news story. And most of all, I couldn't let our lives — my life — be worth nothing anymore.

"We have to take a ride," I said.

My words hung in the air. The thing we swore we'd never do. The thing that, besides pausing the walk or abandoning the walk, would let everyone down. Possibly even more than us quitting altogether. The six words that meant our lives were worth living.

"Fuck," said Anthony.

"Yeah," I said. His f-bomb was his affirmation: he didn't have to lose his life to offer value to the world. He was worth more alive than dead.

So we agreed. We had to take a ride out of the storm. But Anthony was never going to agree to the way I planned to make it happen.

"It gets worse," I said.

"How could it possibly get worse than taking a ride when we swore we wouldn't?" asked Anthony, standing suddenly. He began to pace the floor. "We have to tell people. We're gonna have to let them *know*, and it's going to fucking suck. It calls into question the entire —"

"We have to take a ride...from Rick Lisowsky," I said quietly.

Anthony stared at me. He collapsed onto the bed again, which bounced a bit before settling beneath him. We couldn't *ask* someone for a ride. We couldn't *take* a ride. But we *especially* couldn't ask for, and take, a ride from Rick Lisowsky.

Rick Lisowsky, on permanent disability under the full-time care of his wife, April; Rick Lisowsky, who walked twelve miles with us on the snowy roads near his home in Monument, where his permanent IV was the only thing keeping his body hydrated as he took each step; Rick Lisowsky, the father of two young kids; Rick Lisowsky, whose mom, Deb, had put us up for two whole weeks and fed us and sheltered us and welcomed us around her Thanksgiving table; Rick Lisowsky, the last person on the entire planet you'd ever want to ask for a favor, let alone a huge favor like driving you three hundred miles out of a mountain snowstorm.

"No way," said Anthony. "Not Rick. What are our other options? Can we take a bus or a taxi or something?"

The taxi would have cost more than $300, easy. Even taking a Greyhound bus would have cost $50 to $60 per person, plus we'd have to pay for a taxi to the Greyhound station in

Pueblo, plus we'd lose hours of time — days, even — because the bus would make lots of stops along the way. If the buses were even running during the storm, that is. We didn't have credit cards. Or we didn't have credit cards with any credit left on them. We'd already tapped out our parents and family and friends for donations. It was too shameful to ask for more.

"Okay, what else can we do? Who else do we know around here? What about Matt?" I asked.

"Way too far," said Anthony. "He's all the way up in Denver."

"Ken?" I asked.

"We couldn't," said Anthony. "He just donated the whole meditation course —"

"I know," I said. "He probably could've charged us hundreds of bucks for that. I could only give him, like, ten."

We were silent for a long moment.

"So who else do we know?" I asked, finally.

"Just Deb," said Anthony. "And Rick and April."

I groaned.

We couldn't ask Deb for a ride. It'd be like asking a monk to give you the last grain of rice from his bowl. Rick and April were the only other people we knew in the area. Because of Rick's health problems, April stayed home to take care of him. This meant they were also the only people we knew who wouldn't have to take off work to help us. They could spend the day driving us down to Albuquerque without having to use up vacation days to do it.

No one was crazy about the idea, but when we called him, Rick and his family decided, once again, to help us out. Rick and April would drive down to Pueblo with the kids, pick us up, and drive us through the Raton Pass to Albuquerque. Rick would be tired from the trip, but he'd be okay. If we didn't take a ride, we, on the other hand, would not be.

Once our saviors were en route from Monument, we posted on Facebook and dropped the bomb to our followers. Most people were supportive and understanding of our decision to take a ride. But it's the people who weren't that I remember most.

"You said you wanted to do something hard so you could prove to yourselves you could overcome."

"I thought you said you wouldn't take rides."

"If you take a three-hundred-mile ride, your '2,700-mile trek' will always have an asterisk on it."

In response to the asterisk comment, Anthony wrote, "If that's the case, so be it. I'd rather have an asterisk on the trek than an asterisk on my life."

When Rick's car finally rolled up to our hotel, we got in with our gear. We rode the three hundred or so miles to Albuquerque, out of the storm, away from the snow. It was only when we left Pueblo, Home of Heroes, that I finally *felt* like a hero. It occurred to me then that maybe a hero wasn't someone who blindly sacrificed himself. Maybe a hero was someone who found value and honor in all lives, including his own. Maybe a hero was someone brave enough to do what was right for himself, even when it was wrong for everyone else.

We pooled what little money we had to fill up Rick's tank and buy his family pizza and a hotel room for the night. We thanked them. We thanked them again. We said goodbye. We kept our power. We kept walking, our lives intact, lives that had somehow become worth living for.

26

HOPE

Picture Sergeant Clark alone in the woods. He's blowing up trees to make landing pads for helicopters. He's Aaron Cross alone on the mountain in *The Bourne Legacy* getting rained on by government drones and running from wolves and surviving.

Now see him on top of a moving vehicle in Iraq. See him getting shot at by insurgents. See how he climbs out of the Stryker, past the air guards, screaming bloody murder and firing his weapon as he surfs on top of the hulking vehicle in the dusk. See the wild stare of his blue eyes, the thick, heavy muscles of his chest. Now watch him standing next to Sergeant Diaz on base at Fort Lewis, in the cool wet of Washington State, on the first day I meet him. Watch them stand next to each other — Clark with his white skin and sloping nose and strong chin, Diaz with his receding hairline and shit-eating grin. Watch them together and know they are friends. Watch them laugh and feel how right things are with the world. Feel how brotherhood exists; feel that it exists for you, too. Think of how you're not going to die in Iraq now that Clark and Diaz are here to lead you. Stand in formation in a half circle in the motor pool in your PT uniform so that Clark can inspect you. Watch Clark's eyes as they make contact with yours for the first time. Notice how short he is, how muscular, how he's basically allergic to body fat. Watch as he walks over to you, his eyes narrowing. Look away but listen as he speaks to you for the first time. Listen as he says, "What's up, *Fat Man?*" Listen to your own response as you say, "Nothing, Sergeant." Now listen to your buddy Ethan saying, "Hey, Sergeant, he's alright. He can run and do PT. He's just fat."

Now watch yourself down in plank position, your palms gripping the rocky ground at your base in Iraq. Watch Clark walk away from you, leaving you there to do push-ups till he says stop. Watch him walk past you again forty-five minutes later. Listen to him ask, "Are you still down there?" Translate this to mean your punishment is over. Get up and pick the stones out of the broken skin on your hands.

Watch yourself wake up at 2:00 AM and climb into the room outside Clark's because that's where they keep the radio and you're on radio duty. As you sit down to listen to the radio, watch Clark's shadow moving around in his room. Now watch Clark, standing in the doorway, buck naked, grab his dick and windmill it at you in greeting. Watch him stare right at you as he spins his dick in frantic circles, saying nothing as he works it around and around and around with his hand. Watch him suddenly stop, remove his hand, and go back to bed without a word.

Watch Clark watch you, bewildered by your quiet nature, unsure of what to do with you because you're so unlike him and he doesn't understand you. Maybe because you're just this nice, quiet kid. Realize you were a nice, quiet kid once. Which means that maybe you could get back to that again — who you used to be. Who you really are.

Watch yourself get up early, every day, to ride the stationary bike. Watch Clark nod at you, the slightest sign of approval, when you tell him you're trying — really trying — to lose the weight. Watch Clark stop calling you Fat Man.

Now watch Clark walking out of the office of his first sergeant at the Tactical Operation Center in Mosul, Iraq. Watch him walk over to Ethan. Watch as Ethan pictures himself getting smoked to high heaven or put on extra duty picking up cigarette butts or raking rocks because of what he did. Rewind to Ethan an hour earlier, sweating, as he tells Clark what he did. Then watch sleep-deprived Ethan leaving the chow hall, walking out the door, and forgetting the weapon he'd left propped against the table. Leaving his weapon. Losing his weapon entirely. Watch Ethan brace himself for the punishment of all punishments. Now watch Clark leave his boss's office, pat Ethan on the shoulder, and say, "You're all squared away. Don't let it happen again."

Now stay right there in that moment. Keep moving your feet down the road, but hang on to that moment when Clark is making everything okay. When he's letting everyone off the hook. When he's protecting, defending, advocating for his men. Listen to the sound of his laughter as he walks alongside Sergeant Diaz, who can't stop cracking jokes.

Watch your feet cross New Mexico into Arizona. Listen to

the wind in the trees and watch the sun and clouds make dark shadows on the road ahead. Watch yourself stop, just for a few minutes, to meditate like Ken taught you. Notice yourself start to do that more and more. A few minutes here. A few minutes there. No big deal.

Now watch as a sense of hope begins to bubble beneath the endless earth. Watch hope begin to roar louder than the wind. Watch as hope replaces the pained, ghostlike faces of Clark and Diaz with smiling faces at the height of laughter in happier times. Watch them as their joy peaks like mountains. Let them keep walking alongside each other, alongside you, grounded in the hope that they're still friends in death. That maybe somehow, somewhere, they're together. And they're okay. Listen as hope roars louder than the past. Watch it stop the mouths of the ghosts. Watch it wrap their smiles in a freeze-frame and hold them there forever.

27

IT'S ALL A MIRAGE

Sixty-mile-an-hour winds whipped sand straight into my face. I wiped my eyes with the back of my hand and leaned into the wind. It was so strong, Anthony and I probably could've fallen and let the wind catch us, like some sort of trust exercise at a corporate retreat. A huge, swirling gust caught our packs and pulled them behind us like sails. We could barely move forward. On Route 66 in the heart of the Mojave Desert, there are washout overpasses every few miles. We pushed through the wind as if we were walking through water and took shelter beneath the next bridge.

Gone were the supporters, the press, the film crew, the reliable cell phone reception. Gone was the beauty of Colorado and of New Mexico, where we'd started walking again, in Albuquerque, and eventually made our way across Arizona. Gone was the Painted Desert, with its layered rocks like feathery croissants, its flat-topped peaks and rippling valleys undulating from the earth like frozen russet waves. The Mojave was an ocean of nothingness with an endless highway running through its middle. Days before, somewhere in eastern California, we'd reached the top of a hill. The earth stretched forever in every direction. You could almost see where the planet curved. Like a great, sweeping scar, the highway cut through the land to the horizon. It flattened at the valley floor, then rose again before wrapping around the enormous mountain peak in the distance. The ridge had to be at least ninety miles away — a five-day walk without a change in scenery.

By day we'd fight the wind, every step a small victory. There were no restaurants, no stores, no people in sight. The sky was empty except for a few wispy clouds and the streaks of jet trails, which would hang in the air and spread themselves wider and wider, like stretched cotton, until they disappeared back to nothing. Once, somewhere east of California City, a supporter named Troy Holmes drove out to bring us a bucket of Popeyes chicken. If you're keeping track, this was the second supporter who'd brought us a bucket of chicken to eat while we walked. But mostly we survived on beef jerky and trail mix. At night we'd camp. Around dusk we'd start looking for a good spot off the road that was hidden by a berm or desert brush. We'd spread our packs out, unroll our sleeping bags, take off our boots, and listen to the yips and howls of the coyotes. In the morning we'd grab our boots by the soles, tip them over, and shake them out in case any snakes or scorpions had burrowed there during the night. With my newfound interest in meditation and the resulting peaceful energy that might attract critters, we couldn't be too careful.

Nothing was the something that became the law of the

land. Most of the time, Anthony would walk a few miles ahead of me. His stride was double mine. If we lost sight of each other, he'd stop walking and wait until he saw me again. But we kept our distance. Not much talking. No music, no headphones. No more distractions. And without the typical diversions of the trek — film crew, supporters, social media — the space and time we'd longed for all along, the space and time to confront the past, was finally, undeniably, all around us. In those rare moments when nothing suddenly became something — a car passing us on the road, a dilapidated house with a Keep Out sign, an ancient gas station or abandoned diner — it made our hearts beat faster and our legs push harder against the wind. But usually, in the hours and days and weeks of nothingness that filled in the spaces between the somethings, it was just me, the road, and the boots of Sergeant Clark and Sergeant Diaz keeping pace beside me.

In the great space of nothing, I felt them — and myself — begin to disappear. In the wind I saw demons, memories, lives taken and lost. They emerged through the blowing sand like mirages. They clung to my shoulders, stepped on my feet, showed their faces, only to disappear again into the wind. There's Clark. There's Diaz. There's the man in the black kurta.

Or not.

I couldn't be sure.

Were they even there at all?

They weren't really in the wind, were they? They were in the past. A past that existed only in my mind. Maybe the only things that were real were the wind, the sand, the pain in my feet. And maybe not even those.

I thought a lot about WolfWalker. I rehashed what he said about taking responsibility for my own healing. And how part of taking responsibility was accepting what happened in the past and choosing to learn from it. Knowing there's nothing you can do to change it. For a decade, I'd been a devotee of the dead. I'd lived for them and with them, choosing them over the present moment every time. As if somehow living in the past proved my loyalty to them. My love for them. My regret. As if, by clinging to the past, I could rewrite the story somehow. Like if I kept hanging on to it, I was hanging on to the possibility that I could still change it.

But then I looked ahead, toward the horizon. Two miles down the road, surrounded by desert, dwarfed by a ten-thousand-foot summit, was Anthony — the only time in his life he'd ever looked tiny to anyone. He had walked more than eighteen hundred miles with me. He had listened to my stories and laughed at my jokes. He had shared his own stories and jokes. He was my friend. He was there with me, in that moment, right then. He was alive, right here. Right now.

And there was the sky. I could see it over my head. It wasn't the sky of Kurdistan. It was, for better or worse, the sky somewhere east of Barstow. I could see its blues and grays starting to surrender to the peaches and pinks and oranges of the sunset to come.

And there was the wind. I could feel it pressing into my body, slapping against my skin like God's own wake-up call.

I didn't have the energy to argue anymore about how things should have been. I needed every ounce of energy I had left just to make it through the desert. If I relived the scenes of the past ten thousand times in my mind, it still wouldn't change what happened.

There they were again. Boots on the ground. Clark and Diaz beside me, as always.

I'm sorry, I thought.

I choose Anthony. I choose the sky. I choose the wind.

Forgive me, I thought.

I choose now.

The most important thing when you're walking in the desert is not to get murdered. Or robbed. Especially robbed, because if someone murdered us, we'd just be dead, but if someone robbed us and took our stuff we'd be alive but super fucked. Who's gonna pull over and help a couple of bearded, sweaty, hitchhiker-looking guys in the middle of nowhere in the middle of the desert? No one.

After we'd spent an hour beneath the bridge, the wind died down enough for us to keep going. It was suddenly quiet enough to hear the motor of an oncoming vehicle in the distance. The sound grew louder. We looked back to see an all-in-one camper making its way toward us on the highway. As soon as it passed us, it started to slow down. It pulled to a stop about a mile in front of us. And waited.

As we approached the idling vehicle, the driver rolled down his window. He was a white guy in his sixties, a hippie with a chill burnout vibe that made it feel like we were hitchhiking in the 1960s.

"Hey guys," he said. "What are you up to?"

We told him that we were veterans and we were walking across the country to raise awareness and money and all that.

"Oh, yeah?" he said. "I'm a Vietnam veteran."

"No kidding," we said.

"Where ya walking to?" he asked.

"Santa Monica Pier," we said. "Los Angeles."

"No kidding," he said. "That's where *I'm* heading," he said.

Anthony shot me a look that said, "Okay, either this guy's a serial killer, or this is another crazy coincidence, or the universe is testing us big-time."

"Hop in," said the vet. "I'll give you a ride."

"Thanks, but we can't take rides," said Anthony.

"Okay," said the vet.

He rolled up his window, pulled out onto the highway, and drove away. And drove. And drove. Twenty minutes later, we could still see his camper, ambling down the road past miles and miles that could have been ours — in a car. Now they would still be ours. One painful, solitary step at a time.

Near Barstow, the landscape grew familiar. To the southeast was the Marine Corps Air Ground Combat Center at Twentynine Palms. To the north was the National Training Center at Fort Irwin, where both Anthony and I had spent a month training to go to war before we were first deployed to Iraq. If a wormhole had opened up in the desert, I could have seen myself, ten years younger and just a few miles north of there, learning all the official ways to stay alive in a war zone: never dismount a vehicle by yourself, never turn on vehicle lights at night, and never walk down the road at night with a flashlight looking for IEDs. I could see myself memorizing those rules with all my heart — like if I did a really, really good job studying, just knowing them could somehow keep me alive. *No dismount, no vehicle lights, no flashlights. No dismount, no vehicle lights, no flashlights.*

Through that same ripple in the space-time continuum, I could've watched my sergeant, SFC Gaston — the guy who was supposed to lead us into battle. He was the guy who taught us *no dismount, no vehicle lights, no flashlights.* He was the guy who, during one of our training exercises, *dismounted his vehicle, turned on his vehicle lights,* and *turned on his flashlight to start looking for IEDs.* I could've watched the ensuing ambush and dozens of my friends marked for dead on the ground. I could've watched the relief in younger-me's eyes the next morning when we found out SFC Gaston was no longer assigned to our platoon and wouldn't be coming with us to Iraq.

I'd stand at attention while the platoon leader said, "Meet your new platoon sergeant and squad leader. This is Sergeant Clark," he said. "Your new platoon sergeant. And this is Sergeant Diaz," he said. "Your new squad leader."

I'd watch Clark take command of our platoon with a steadfast, wild-eyed stare. I'd know, just by the look in his eye, that he was the most badass noncommissioned officer I'd ever met. I'd know he was a total hardass, totally nuts, and that to him, being a good leader meant taking a bullet for any one of us in a heartbeat.

I'd watch Diaz grinning in the background. I'd watch him lean in, whisper something to Clark, and make him laugh when no one else could. I'd think how it took just as much confidence and bravery to be friends with Clark as it did to lead a platoon. In this way, Clark and Diaz were equally brave. They were peers. They were brothers.

I'd watch my younger self breathe a sigh of relief.

"Thank God," I'd see myself thinking as I looked at the two of them, laughing. "I'm not going to die."

Because of them, or maybe because of God, or maybe for a reason I'll never know, I didn't.

I didn't die.

I lived.

I had the chance they no longer had. I owed it to them to step fully and finally into the world of now, the place they couldn't be. And I couldn't do that with boots on the ground in Iraq, or Fort Irwin, or Fort Lewis, or Fort Benning. I couldn't do that from the bottom of a bottle. I could only do it then and there. In the Mojave. Where the nothingness enveloped everything — even the past. Even them.

And then I realized I had been wrong all along about the ghosts of Clark and Diaz. They hadn't been following me around since Iraq. They hadn't been haunting me and tormenting me like I'd thought. They hadn't been unable to let me go. It had been *me* who'd been hanging on to *them*. Every time I saw or felt them, they'd been trying to help me, not hurt me. They'd been pushing me in the direction of healing so I might finally let them go. Diaz in the bar that night, telling me I'd hit rock bottom, telling me to go see Beck, to tell her I couldn't take it anymore, to tell her I needed to change or I was going to end my life. Diaz and Clark at the start of the walk, standing beside me, committing to walk with me until I was strong enough to walk on my own. And in the desert, across the miles, where the heat and wind and sky made it undeniably clear that I was there, I was not dead, I was alive. They were telling me I was supposed to be alive. They were supposed to be dead. As long as I clung to their memories, wishing things had been different, resisting the past, they'd never be at peace. If I loved them, I had to let them go. Not just for me, but for them. So their souls could finally stop babysitting mine; so they could finally rest and be at peace.

And so I let them go in the desert. First Staff Sergeant Diaz. Then Master Sergeant Clark. With grace and mercy, their ghosts floated away from me like freed birds — Diaz's mustache became eagle feathers. Clark's eyes, the eyes of a hawk. And then they were nothing, just one with the wind and sky.

Thank you, I thought, and then, *I'm sorry*.

And finally, I thought, *Goodbye*.

Relief washed over me in wave upon wave of gratitude. Ethan's rucksack suddenly felt ten pounds lighter.

I kept walking.

28

SHAKEY TOWN

Troy Holmes's house was in Canyon Country, in Santa Clarita, California, about forty miles northwest of LA proper. We stayed with him for thirteen nights as we made our way from Barstow to Santa Monica. In the evenings, Troy would come pick us up wherever we happened to stop walking. He'd drive us all the way back to his house so we could shower and eat dinner. Then we'd all walk down the block to the VFW, where veterans from every generation would buy us drinks until we were drunk. The next day, Troy would drive us to wherever we'd left off, and we'd start walking again from there.

Walking in Los Angeles was different from walking anywhere else we'd been. The city hummed beneath and between endless freeways that crisscrossed like cement spaghetti, a jungle of intersecting pathways packed with millions of cars driven by millions of road-raging citizens. We were never sure exactly where the city started, or if we were finally, really there. It felt like we never really *arrived* because there *was* no Los Angeles. There was just Pasadena and Palmdale, Glendale and Burbank, Mid-Wilshire and Westwood and Venice. Maybe Hollywood was Los Angeles, or maybe downtown LA was Los Angeles. It was a city of cities, a patchwork quilt of neighborhoods demarcated by the cost to live there, the people who lived there, the ease with which you could or couldn't park there. It was the city of your own perspective: all soft and dreamy and filled with possibility and promise or hard and fake and soul-sucking, where it couldn't care less if you stayed or left. Whether dreamy or punishing, it was, for all, a city of unrequited love, where most dreams didn't come true and even the ones that did, didn't last.

LA was where our journey ended because it was where Route 66 officially ended. The end of the road was marked by the ocean, but also by a sign that said "Route 66 — End of the Trail" that was placed, somewhat cheekily, on Santa Monica Pier. It was the place I'd imagined when I first dreamed up the trek all those months ago in Beck's apartment — the end of the line, the point that marked the completion of a long, arduous journey that finished at the water's edge.

We reached the intersection of Hollywood and Vine — 12.6 miles from the finish line — on January 31, 2014. The place was packed with an energized, almost sexualized sense of desperation: regular people desperate for a glimpse of someone famous; locals who desperately wanted to *be* famous; people ogling the camera crew following us and wondering if *we* were famous. It was ironic that this was the place tourists came to experience LA. When Beck lived there, she raved about the city's natural beauty — how you could hike Runyon Canyon for mountain views in the middle of the city or hike past the Tree of Life that overlooked the sea in Will Rogers Park or see all the lights of the San Fernando Valley shimmering at night where the 405 crested northward over the mountain. And she'd never shut up about the food. She couldn't get enough of the packed Mexican cantinas and the $5 sushi happy hours and the twenty-four-hour pho places and the build-your-own burger joints. She had top ten lists for Thai food and knew every deli and brunch spot, from North Hollywood to Laguna Beach.

I saw none of that. Instead I saw a wax museum and a bar with blacked-out windows and a specialty shoe store just for strippers. I saw a Hard Rock Cafe and tour buses and T-shirt shops that looked just like the Hard Rock Cafe and tour buses and T-shirt shops in Las Vegas or Times Square. Anthony and I walked past the big mall at Hollywood and Highland Avenue and stepped on the stars on the Walk of Fame. We saw out-of-work actors in Batman and SpongeBob costumes working for tips. We saw American and European and Chinese tourists taking selfies in front of Mann's Chinese Theatre and rappers trying to sell CDs to passersby.

As we wove through people on the packed sidewalks, Michael and the crew followed behind us in a rental car, with the camera sticking out the window. When traffic slowed down, he'd lose sight of us and jump out of the car and run after us to get the shot he wanted. He'd call out to us, asking us to slow down. A few times, we pretended not to hear him. The air of desperation, the hustlers and tourists, the dinge and grime that clung to the surface of the streets, the funk of stale beer in the air outside empty bars, the sex toy shops, the way the exhaust and heat of the sun got trapped between the buildings and filled my lungs with the stench of warm cement: it all felt dirty. We wanted to get out of there as fast as possible.

Anthony and I pushed forward, struggling through the crowd of tourists. One of the rapper-entrepreneurs selling CDs approached Anthony.

"Hey, man, I want to give you this CD. Check it out," he said.

"Thanks," said Anthony. "I'll give it a listen."

I shot Anthony a look that said, "You're never going to listen to that. And who listens to CDs anymore? It's 2014."

Anthony took the CD from the rapper anyway, and we continued to elbow our way along the wide, packed sidewalk in front of the Chinese Theatre.

The rapper followed us. "Hey, man, that's ten dollars," he said.

"What?" said Anthony, spinning around to face the guy. "You said you were *giving* it to me," he argued.

The verbal altercation that followed led Anthony to post on Facebook that Hollywood was a terrible place full of "degenerates and hustlers."

The grit of Hollywood Boulevard where it crosses Vine and Highland soon gave way to the swank of West Hollywood and the Sunset Strip. We walked past designer boutiques, where shopgirls modeled skin-tight jeggings in doorways; swank hotels with rooftop swimming pools; open-air cafés and secret jazz clubs in back rooms where you had to be on the list to get in; gay bars and straight bars and in-between bars and Sprinkles Cupcakes and Pink's Hot Dogs and packed Jewish delis.

And then we crossed into Beverly Hills, and suddenly

everything was green. The lawns were soft and lime-colored, and the giant palm trees swayed and sparkled in the sun. Immaculate homes were hidden behind perfectly manicured hedges. Fountains danced in the courtyards of iconic hotels: Beverly Hills. Beverly Hilton. Beverly Wilshire.

Anthony and I strolled down the boulevard, past guards in little booths whose job it was to keep nonresidents out of the gated communities. But sometimes I could see the houses from the street, and when I could, I noticed crews of people tending to the great, green lawns. Every lawn we saw had workers scattered about, trimming the hedges, mowing the lawn, spraying plants with a spray gun attached to a *Ghostbusters*-style backpack. There were dozens of them, four or six guys at every house we passed that we could see. They were pruning and sweeping and blowing and mowing, caring for the land, out in the sun, underneath the silently swaying palms with shiny leaves. I wondered where the owners of the homes were at that moment, and what they were doing so they could afford to hire so many people to take such good care of their houses.

As we tromped along the sidewalk, our dirty clothes and sweaty beards painfully out of place, I thought about Wolf-Walker. I remembered what he'd said about taking responsibility for your own healing, and how no one else can do it for you, how you can't outsource the restoration of your soul. I imagined that the people who outsourced their landscaping, and their childcare, and their errand-running, and their dog-walking also had personal assistants and press agents and stylists and a team of people helping them run the business of being them. Maybe, just like they left the care of their home to other people, they left the care of their soul to others, too. Through private yoga instructors and masseurs and life coaches and meditation teachers, they tried to outsource their well-being.

I looked at the marble and stucco and wrought iron and gold and thought about how I had no home to go back to. I looked at the men trimming the hedges and realized I had more in common with them than I did with the faceless, fabulous homeowners. I didn't know how to get rich or how to be famous or who to make deals with or how to be successful. I couldn't even imagine the lives those people were leading behind the doors that had been imported from France. But I was pretty sure that by now, 2,691 miles into the trek, I had learned something important — that one of the secrets to happiness and healing was to trim your own hedges. To tend to the parts of you that grow wild and unwieldy without regular attention and care. To take responsibility for the parts of yourself that need to be tamed and revitalized on the regular. Deep, true, lasting healing can't come from anyone but you.

At the end of the day, Troy Holmes came and picked me up in Beverly Hills. Holly and Madeline, who'd flown in from Wisconsin, picked up Anthony, and they all went to stay together in a hotel.

That night, Troy treated all of us — me, Anthony, Holly, Madeline, and the entire film crew — to dinner at a fancy Italian restaurant in Hollywood. At one point during dinner, I stepped outside to get some air and saw Ron Jeremy, the porn star, driving a late-'90s forest-green Saturn slowly down Las Palmas Avenue. He pulled over and stuck his mustache out the window at me.

"Hey!" said Ron Jeremy. "Do you know where Arena Stage is?"

I looked at the white cement building directly across the street from us. It boasted not one, not two, but four prominently placed signs across its facade, two of which read Arena in big, black lettering.

"Looks like it's right here," I said to Ron Jeremy.

"Thanks!" he said, relieved, and drove away.

I spent the last night of the trek alone in Troy's house. As I lay on the couch and tried to sleep, I was overcome with amazement and unease. I had practically done it — finished the biggest, craziest thing I'd ever set out to do. It was incredible, it was healing, and in just a few more hours and a few more miles, it would be over.

29

REUNION

Anthony and I were seven miles from the finish line when I rounded a bend in Beverly Gardens Park and saw Ethan standing in the sun. It had been more than four years since I'd seen him. In that time, he'd met Stephanie, gotten married, become a father, and was now expecting his second child. His wife stood next to him on the soft, sandy hiking path that ran parallel to Santa Monica Boulevard. She was tall like Ethan, with long, dark hair and a taut, pregnant belly. The two of them were greeting Anthony with wide smiles when I spotted them.

Ethan always looked slightly different from the image I had of him in my mind. To me he was perpetually twenty-six years old, with the lean trunk and narrow neck of a college track star. He was older now — still fit, but sturdier somehow, like his body had widened to support the load of marriage and parenthood. The vertical crease between his eyebrows had deepened, but I knew that beneath his baseball cap and behind his dark sunglasses, his eyes looked the same as they had in Iraq — crinkled around the edges, like he was wise beyond his years.

Ethan wore a T-shirt with our platoon's insignia on it — a skull and crossbones, set on top of an arrowhead, centered on an ace of spades playing card. Above the skull and crossbones were the words "We Who Do Not Die." Like Ethan, I'd know that symbol anywhere, no matter how long it'd been since I'd last seen it. I recognized its shape and its irony. Many of us did die, in the war or when we got home. I recognized it for its truth; we all lived on forever in the hearts and minds of those who survived.

"Hey, what's up?" I greeted Ethan.

We embraced.

"You're almost done?" asked Ethan, grinning.

"Seven miles, and we're done."

Michael had chosen Beverly Gardens Park as a meeting point because the lush lawn and big fountain and plentiful palms created a cinematic backdrop for my reunion with Ethan, who was there to walk the last stretch of the trek with us. The sky was somehow a deeper, richer blue than it had been elsewhere in the city. The cement and storefronts were replaced with thick, rustling palm fronds, running water, and emerald nature all around us. The sun so yellow, the temperature so perfect as to be undetectable, our smiles taking agency over our faces without our consent. Ethan said goodbye to Stephanie, who'd meet us at the finish line later in the day. It must have been something about the angle of their bodies as they parted, the ease with which they leaned toward each other, the way Ethan let his cheek press briefly against her temple to say goodbye that made me realize how in love they were. I glanced over as he kissed her goodbye beneath the blue sky in the green park, and I wanted to stay in that moment forever. I wanted Ethan and Stephanie to stay that happy and sheepish and pregnant and proud for-fucking-ever. I believed that if Ethan could stay that happy for the rest of his life, it would make up for the death of the girl in Iraq.

It was chaotic in Baghdad that day. Ethan was in the Doura neighborhood. Squads were clearing here and there. Ethan's platoon had been chasing a target, his sniper team on overwatch. He looked down the road and saw a man covered in blood carrying a child. He grabbed the medic and brought the man and the dying girl into their overwatch house. The house owner tried to shoo the man out. But Ethan brought them in anyway and treated the girl right there on the floor of the house. Ethan cut away her shirt and found a puncture wound in her chest. He didn't have an interpreter, so he had no idea how the girl had been injured and couldn't ask. He and the medic sealed the wound in her chest as the girl gasped for one last breath. The men of the house stood around them in a circle. They were garbed in white. He didn't know the name for the little round caps they wore on their heads. The man who brought the girl into the house stood with them, covered in her blood.

The girl's pulse stopped shortly after her breathing did. As Ethan moved her limbs, he could still feel life in them. They weren't quite limp yet. The medic got out his CPR mask, and they started two-person CPR: ten compressions, two breaths for a child. The men of the house began praying in Arabic. All Ethan could make out was Allah-something, he wasn't quite sure. After a little while, they stopped doing CPR. The girl was dead. Ethan tried to mime to the man in blood that she was dead, but he wasn't quite sure how to communicate it. He motioned his hand over her body and looked straight into the man's eyes. It wasn't even her father who'd found her.

Ethan and the medic covered the body, and the man in blood carried her out of the cordoned house. Ethan had called up the situation, but the platoon was too busy searching for a combatant, so the girl's life passed without notice. Ethan was sick as he thought of the girl's lifeless body on the floor. He was sure the search going on all around him was meaningless, just like her death. I wanted our reunion, and his family, and the yellow sun and blue sky to take the memory away, or to soften it in his mind, or to make it all mean something, somehow.

Anthony, Ethan, and I walked west along Santa Monica Boulevard, toward the sea. As we walked, the film crew all around us, we told Ethan about Abraham Lincoln in Iowa and WolfWalker in Colorado. We told him about the meditation class and Raton Pass and the Mojave. We told him about getting Popeyes chicken delivered to us, twice, and how a Vietnam vet offered to give us a ride all the way to Santa Monica.

We stopped at an intersection so that Anthony and I could give an interview to a couple of local reporters.

"How many *outfits* did you bring?" asked the first reporter.

"I don't know," I said. "Like, three T-shirts and two pairs of pants."

"Did you lose *weight*?" asked the other.

"Not really," I said.

That was all they asked.

30

WAVE

Two miles from the finish line, I started to feel like Forrest Gump. I remembered the part in the movie where he "just felt like running" and started running across the country, back and forth, from East Coast to West. Eventually, other people started running with him, a few at first, and then more and more. That's kind of what happened to me and Anthony on the last day of the trek. With our long beards that hadn't been trimmed since Milwaukee, we even sort of looked like Forrest during that part of the movie.

A bunch of guys from a veteran biker gang called the Booze-fighters walked with us. Then there was the brother of a Milwaukee vet who'd taken us to dinner in Nebraska. Then there was a meditation teacher Michael knew who was going on and on about a meditation workshop created just for veterans. In just a couple of weeks, Anthony and I had gone from being the only human beings for miles in the big, empty desert, to being surrounded by a crowd and flanked by a film crew in the middle of one of the most famous cities in the world.

The whole lot of us made our way down Santa Monica Boulevard until it intersected Ocean Avenue, and there it was — the ocean! Beyond the rows of perfect palm trees, beneath the brown bluffs, past the 10 freeway that became US-1 that became Pacific Coast Highway far below, and beyond the wide parking lots and white sand beach, was the ocean we'd covered 2,700 miles to see.

We took a sharp left and walked down Ocean Avenue. Homeless people lounged on benches and slept in tents they'd pitched in the lime-green manicured park overlooking the water. I wondered how many of them were veterans.

Anthony's family was waiting for him on the pier, along with every major news outlet in Los Angeles. His wife, his daughter, his job were all waiting for him when he got back home — a home he was ready to go back to. In those last moments of the trek, the thing we'd given every ounce of energy and time and resources to over the past eight months, I was becoming painfully aware that I wasn't ready for it to end. Not only had I not healed everything that needed healing, but I wasn't sure what I had to go back to.

To get to Santa Monica Pier from the park, we had to walk along an overpass above the Pacific Coast Highway. Michael had set up a camera on the pier to get a shot of us walking down the overpass ramp. Half of the crew filmed us from the pier. The rest followed us down the ramp with a handheld camera, expertly weaving in and out of the moving crowd. They weren't alone; in addition to the huge crowd that was following us by that point, plus the group of reporters who were following us down the rampway toward the pier, was another film crew that was following none other than Chris Abele, the Milwaukee County executive who'd promised us another $10,000 for finishing the trek. Abele's flight from Milwaukee to Los Angeles for the end of the walk had been canceled at the last minute. He couldn't get on another commercial flight in time, so he'd chartered a private jet.

"What's going on?" I heard someone ask as we passed with reporters and film crews trailing.

"That guy from the *Hangover* is filming something here today," someone else responded. I wondered if they thought me or Anthony looked more like comedian Zach Galifianakis.

We cut through cameras and reporters, who swarmed around us like locusts. Ethan, the Boozefighters, and other supporters fell behind as Anthony and I neared the finish line — the tall, black-and-white highway sign that read "Santa Monica 66 — End of the Trail." It was the official end of the old Route 66, and the official end of Veterans Trek. At the end of the pier, a firefighter lifted his radio to his mouth. "Go ahead," he said into the radio. A fireboat began to move toward the pier. Members of the fire department used a giant hose to shoot water into the air like a cannon. Anthony and I stood there and watched them give us a salute. Then we posed for pictures with all the other veterans who were there.

It was February 1, 2014 — five months, two days, and

2,700* miles from our send-off at the war memorial by the water in Milwaukee. We had done it. We had walked across the country, and we were done.

After posing for pictures with other vets and answering the reporters' questions, Anthony and I broke away from the crowd. We walked past the Bubba Gump Shrimp Company and the Ferris wheel and Whac-A-Mole stands and walked beyond the finish line to the end of the pier. We looked out at the water in silence.

"Welp, we did it," said Anthony, after some time. "We're done."

"Yep," I said.

And that was all we said about that.

Anthony went off with his family, and for a moment I was alone, grateful for the anonymous crowd of tourists that shielded me from the cameras and questions. The questions were all the same, anyway. They were always some version of, "How does it feel to be done?" And my answers, predictable, were always some version of, "Good. It feels good to be done."

When I leaned over the railing and looked straight ahead at the horizon, it was exactly as I had imagined it nearly a year before in Beck's apartment. I was standing on Santa Monica Pier, staring at the Pacific Ocean. I was leaning on the railing at the end of the pier until I could see nothing but the sea. And

---

* The ride we took from Pueblo, Colorado, to just outside Albuquerque, New Mexico, was around 340 miles. That means we walked about 2,358 miles of the 2,700 miles we traveled. We are forever grateful we got out of the storm — and for this asterisk.

as I looked at it, I could imagine an endless sea inside me, an expanse as great as the ocean. I still had a soul. It was a big soul. It was so big that it was connected to everything and everyone. It was just like WolfWalker said back in Colorado. I wasn't separate from the ocean or the people on the pier. I was a part of things. I had reclaimed my place in the world of the living.

The coastline was shaped like a crescent moon with me at its center. To the northwest I could see the faint white strips of Malibu's beaches across the great bay. To the south thin layers of distant land rose from the sea. The ocean had an energy, a spirit, a life force that I could feel and sense with every cell of my body. There was no difference between the life force that was keeping me alive and the life force that made waves ripple over the surface of the sea. We were made of the same stuff. And so we were one.

I saw waves scattered across the sea, stretching, yearning to separate from the larger body. I imagined they wanted to be free and distinct and that was why they rose up. And as they peaked, it suddenly dawned on them that to separate themselves from the ocean was to end themselves. So they'd fall back into oneness, merging once more. And the whole of them would rush toward land, then retreat, then rush toward land again, each time forgetting the lesson they'd learned the last time they made a break for it.

The sense of connection passed as quickly as it came. Like the waves, I again felt the pull of separation, the dream of it. Almost immediately, my worries and fears about the walk coming to an end rose to the surface.

I healed on the walk, sure. But did I heal enough?

Was the walk even worth it, if I'm not completely healed? I said that if five months and 2,700 miles weren't enough to heal me, nothing was. Did I fail?

With each breaking wave, a new wave of worry arose in my mind.

I have no job. What am I going to do for work when I get back to Milwaukee?

Where am I going to live?

How will I pay the bills?

For the past five months, I'd been completely focused on healing. I was doing nothing but walking and thinking and hoping for relief. My only concern was excavating and examining this soul-wound-thing inside me and supporting other vets who were doing the same. What would happen when I had to work a regular job, and deal with people, and spend most of my energy trying to have a normal life without the suicide tape in my head starting up again?

What if the trek was my one shot to deal with my shit, and I came up short?

I turned my back on the water. I could see Anthony through the crowd, smiling at Holly. He had Madeline up on his shoulders. I couldn't see Ethan, but I knew he was there in the crowd with Stephanie, waiting for me. We'd go to dinner with everyone: Anthony and Holly, Michael and Jerry and Melissa, Ethan and Stephanie, and Chris Abele, who'd pay for it all. We'd drink those giant fishbowl drinks they sell on the pier. Then Ethan would drive me up to Santa Barbara, where I'd stay with his family for a few days and finally give him back his rucksack. They were all waiting for me to get the celebration started.

But what was waiting for me?

Part 3

STILL

The fire of knowledge burns all karmas to ashes.

— Bhagavad Gita

31

THE UNNAMEABLE THING

At first I didn't think much of the two emails that landed in my in-box that spring, one right after the other. I thought they were worth a quick read, sure. But they were just emails. Not a huge deal. And certainly nothing that would matter in the ultimate scheme of things.

Anthony and I had driven back across the country the way we had come, retracing thousands of miles in a rental car. What was waiting for me back home was half a dozen homecoming celebrations, both public and private, that climaxed, then fizzled, into a mundane, everyday existence in much the same way that coming home from deployment had: odd jobs cutting trees in the cold because I couldn't stand the thought of working in an office again after spending five months outside in the great drama of the great outdoors, enveloped in what WolfWalker had called "everything that is around us," becoming a part of that, becoming myself in that. And these emails, one from Michael Collins, and the other from a woman, a veteran and an officer whose name I can't even remember.

Isn't it funny how the most important moments of your life can pass you by, practically unnoticed? Like having an unremarkable first meeting with a person who later becomes your spouse. Or not being in the mood for sex that results in conception. Or having a meeting pushed back by fifteen minutes, which makes you leave work fifteen minutes later than usual, which leaves you stuck in traffic so you avoid a car accident that otherwise would have killed you. It's like not remembering the name of the person who invited you to a workshop that would shift the entire course of your life.

March 18, 2014. One of the directors of photography for the documentary, Melissa, wasn't traveling or in production, so she was at home in the Brooklyn apartment she shared with her boyfriend. Because she'd been working on the documentary with Michael and Jerry, she'd been reading everything she could about veterans and PTSD. She'd gotten into the habit of sending Michael and Jerry articles she found interesting and relevant to the project. That day Melissa sent Michael and Jerry a link to a three-part series of articles written by David Wood for *The Huffington Post*, "A Warrior's Moral Dilemma."

When he got Melissa's email, Michael read each of the articles, one right after the other. Then he sent the articles to Anthony and me.

I hadn't been checking email that regularly. The trek was over, and I was working outside, so I didn't really need to. But for some reason, on that day I checked. As I clicked through each article, words and phrases leapt from the screen, jumping into parts of my mind and heart, naming things that until then had remained nameless.

"When right and wrong are hard to tell apart..."

"Moral confusion..."

"I'm a good person and yet I've done bad things..."

"They are proud but uneasy... They are not okay... Their fundamental understanding of right and wrong has been violated... by the moral and ethical ambiguities of war... Damned if they kill, damned if they don't... Moral injury is a relatively new concept... Moral injury."

Moral injury.

Moral injury.

Wood defined it as "a relatively new concept that seems to describe what many feel: a sense that their fundamental understanding of right and wrong has been violated, and the grief, numbness or guilt that often ensues."

Moral injury!

It was the wound-to-the-soul thing, the not-just-PTSD-thing, the thing that kept me up nights.

It was the unnameable thing that finally had a name.

For Michael, Melissa, and the crew, moral injury was the framework they needed to shape all the footage they'd shot for the documentary. Throughout all our interviews, all the footage, Michael knew Anthony and I weren't just talking about PTSD. He knew the puzzle we were trying to solve wasn't just physical or psychological but moral, even spiritual, in nature. But, just like us, and just like so many veterans, he hadn't known exactly what to call it.

As I trimmed trees in the frigid spring, healed in part by a 2,700-mile journey, more responsible for my part in that healing process, less afraid to face the past, still afraid to face the past, still afraid any progress I'd made could be undone at any moment, the thing at the heart of it all had a name. When I was diagnosed with PTSD, it felt like a puzzle with the central piece missing. Moral injury was the missing piece. Yes, I had PTSD from my time in war. But PTSD was just one part of the story. Moral injury, with its focus on shame, guilt, sorrow, and grief, felt much more accurate. It helped tell the whole story. If I could name the unnameable thing inside me, if I could look at it and categorize it and dissect it, if I could talk to other people about it and hear their thoughts about it, maybe it would be easier to heal.

The second seemingly insignificant email I got that spring actually kind of annoyed me at first. It was from a veteran, an officer in the army. She was organizing a meditation workshop for vets in Aspen, Colorado. She wondered if I wanted to come out and take the course. The workshop would be taught by Ken and James — the same Ken who'd taught our four-day meditation course in Colorado, and the same James who'd walked the last few miles of the trek with us in Santa Monica, talking my ear off about an upcoming meditation course he thought I should take. This was that course.

Even more synchronistic was the fact that the course in Aspen was the same course Anthony had taken a few years ago in Madison; if I took it, I'd be learning the same meditation and breathing techniques Anthony had learned before the trek. It was the course he'd done as part of a research study, and it too had been taught by James. It was the course that created feelings of relief and joy akin to "smoking a whole joint at your favorite band's concert during an extended jam," according to Anthony. It was the course that introduced Anthony to Michael, back when Michael was first thinking about making a film about veterans. So I was being invited to take the same course that had connected Anthony to Michael, Michael to me, and me to WolfWalker, Ken, and James — all of which led to the email that was sitting in my in-box, waiting to be answered.

But all I saw when I opened that email was an invitation to take a meditation course I couldn't possibly afford to take.

Thanks, I wrote back, irritated, *but no thanks.*

I just got back from five months on the road, so I haven't been working for the past five months. There's just no way I can afford to take more time off, let alone pay for a plane ticket and a ride from Aspen to Denver and a hotel room and everything else. I appreciate the invite, but maybe next time.

I pressed Send and didn't give the workshop a second thought.

Until a few weeks later, when the officer wrote back.

Hey, Tom, good news! An anonymous donor has offered to fly all the veterans on the course to Aspen. We'll provide you with a ride from Denver to Aspen, pay for your hotel, and all your meals will be included. I realize this would still mean taking five days off work, and that it might be hard to get the time off. But the out-of-pocket cost to you would be $0 for the course. You would need to share your hotel room with a roommate — another combat vet. So that's something to consider, too. Hope to hear from you soon.

32

FLASH

Ken had no idea he was driving Trevor and me absolutely crazy.

At the baggage claim in the Denver airport, my new friend Trevor and I had watched Ken scanning the crowd for us. When he'd finally spotted us, he'd smiled a warm, Mr. Rogers smile. The three of us had walked together toward the parking lot, where Ken's SUV was waiting to drive us to Aspen. Trevor was a marine, a fellow combat vet, and my roommate for the five-day meditation course. As we left the arrivals area, I'd scanned the airport for signs of Michael and the film crew he'd hired to document the workshop.

"It's funny," said Michael, when I told him I was taking the meditation course. "I thought we were done filming."

"Aren't we?" I asked, confused.

"But now we know that the story isn't over yet," Michael said. "Even though we've known intuitively the kind of work you've been doing to heal yourself, we now have the concept of moral injury to help guide the conversation about it. And what better setting to talk about that than a meditation workshop, which you're taking to actually heal moral injury?"

I agreed to talk about moral injury on camera. It seemed like the thread that tied everything in the film together — it was the reason Anthony and I had gone on the walk. It was the wound we hadn't been able to place. It was the reason the PTSD diagnosis and the EMDR therapy and the medications hadn't worked for me — because the injuries inflicted in war had taken place on a spiritual level and needed to be healed at that level, too. I still didn't know how I was gonna do that. I still thought what happened in the desert, where I finally let go of Clark and Diaz, was just luck, but at least I knew what the problem was. And I knew that there had to be other vets out there like me, whose PTSD diagnosis just wasn't getting to the core of what was wrong inside.

But I was hardly expecting any kind of magical break-through or sudden shift in perspective that warranted a whole *film crew* being there. If I'd learned one thing during the trek, it was that healing takes time. It happens in small, meaningful ways, not mind-blowing revelations or explosions of under-standing and relief. The only way to heal moral injury was to patch the wound, one stitch at a time. And that kind of slow, steady, patient progress sure didn't seem to me the stuff rivet-ing movies were made of. But Michael seemed sure, so I shrugged and went with it.

Trevor and I hopped into Ken's Isuzu. As we pulled out of the airport and inserted ourselves into the mountainous stretches between Denver and Aspen, the familiarity of the landscape made it feel like another kind of homecoming. I was back in nature, in the peaks and valleys of the mountains, and back on the road, moving through space and time, moving through trauma, moving away from the past. I was right where I belonged.

The distance from Denver to Aspen was more than 150 miles. Ken drove along I-70 and then cut south toward Aspen. I kept waiting for him to turn on the radio, but he didn't. Trevor and I shot the shit about our mutual deployments and the jobs we'd had in the military. But that took up only a few minutes. So the three of us drove in silence — for hours.

After what felt like an eternity, Ken slowed the car and pulled to a grinding, painful halt behind hundreds of other cars that were stopped outside a closed tunnel.

"Sometimes this tunnel is closed," said Ken. "Let's turn on the radio real quick and listen to the news to see what's happening."

Once Ken heard that the tunnel was backed up because of an accident, he snapped the radio back off and silence filled the car again — only this time, the silent car was stopped dead in gridlock traffic.

I wanted to crawl out of my skin.

I used music in the car the way I used alcohol. I used it to numb and cover up what was going on inside my head. If I gave my brain something to latch on to, it was much easier to avoid feelings of anxiety or troubling thoughts. That's why Anthony and I vowed not to listen to music on the trek; we thought it would distract us from the exact stuff we wanted to face.

But there, in a traffic jam outside a tunnel in Colorado, I

suddenly understood the difference between being stuck in a silent car and walking outside. Outside, there's always some sort of music, whether it's the sounds of birds or the wind rustling in the leaves or the sound of your own heartbeat. On the road, you could physically step through the thoughts of the past and the anxiety for the future. In the car, there was no escaping myself, no moving through it. I felt trapped with myself, with no way out, like a raccoon trying to claw its way out of a garbage can.

Being stuck in the silent car with no end in sight also sucked because I was a combat vet. I was hardwired from my military service to be a mission-oriented person. I always wanted to know where we were going, how we were getting there, and how long it would take. In combat, everyone *has* to know what's going on at all times. If they don't, people can get hurt or killed. So not knowing how long we'd be stuck in traffic or when the tunnel would open or when we'd get to Aspen began to trigger all sorts of panic. Plus, I was sitting still, in absolute silence, going out of my mind, while everyone else (or maybe just Ken) seemed *perfectly fine with it*. And then, to make it even worse, I realized I was about to spend *five days* sitting still in absolute silence, which seemed absolutely ridiculous since I couldn't even stand to sit in a silent car for *three hours*.

By the time we got to Aspen, my knuckles were white, and my body was so tense I felt like I was bracing to be hit by an oncoming car. I practically leapt out of Ken's SUV and into the hotel lobby, where I was greeted by several vets who were there to take the course, too. They were strangers, but because of our shared service, they were instantly family to me. The familiar bonds of brother- and sisterhood eased the anxiety of the road. Even though we were in the lobby of the Limelight Hotel, meeting them made it feel like coming home.

I don't know what I expected to have happen during the workshop, but it certainly wasn't what actually happened. I guess I thought it'd be like Ken's class, 2.0. We'd sit, we'd breathe in and out, and maybe I'd experience a subtle sense of clarity and calm when the whole thing was said and done. Maybe some deer would even come to the hotel windows and blow our minds for a moment or two.

When it was time to start the course, we all sat on hotel banquet chairs in a semicircle, facing Ken and James. A lot of the other vets had combat injuries that made it difficult for them to sit on the floor, so we all sat in the chairs to make it more comfortable for everyone. I followed the instructions Ken and James gave. I closed my eyes. I breathed in and out. I tried to watch my thoughts come and go instead of getting swept away by them.

We'd meditate all morning. Then, in the afternoons, we'd hike in the national forests surrounding Aspen. One time the group went ice-skating, but I sat out. Sometimes I'd just go rest in my room because the breath work seemed to take a lot out of me. I felt myself coming down with a terrible cold, which made breathing through my nose really hard. All in all, it was okay. I was glad to be there, at least. But it was nothing special.

Until the third day.

On the third day, we learned a special breathing technique that was different from anything we'd learned before. This technique involved breathing in certain patterns, slow breaths followed by medium breaths followed by super fast breaths, that sort of thing. We listened to the breathing pattern and followed along to a tape.

I was sitting in one of the banquet chairs with my eyes closed and the backs of my hands resting on my thighs. The tape changed patterns, and we all started to do the super fast breathing. Suddenly, flashes of light and color appeared in my mind's eye. These flashes were like quick cuts in a movie. They were so vivid, it felt like I was watching an actual film. They were happening so fast that I didn't even have time to wonder what I was watching. I wasn't trying to make them happen; I wasn't even thinking about anything in particular. But there they were — scenes from Iraq, all of them. I saw myself getting blown up. I saw civilians dead in the street. I saw my platoon getting mortared and attacked, and then explosions everywhere. One scene after another in rapid succession. Flash! Flash! Flash!

Then, as quickly as they'd come, the scenes were gone.

After we finished the meditation, we all opened our eyes and talked about our experience that day. I didn't share what had happened because I didn't really *know* what had happened. And before I even had time to think about it, I noticed Michael loitering in the hallway outside the hotel conference room. The patterned breathing part of the workshop was supposed to be super private so that everyone could feel comfortable processing whatever came up for them. They wanted us to feel free to fully experience the emotions that came up, however they came up. Michael and the crew had to wait in the hallway, and no cameras were allowed.

Michael had come back to the hotel to take me on a field trip that James had arranged. I felt drained from the special breathing we'd learned, baffled by the experience I'd had during the session, and sick with one of the worst head colds I'd had in my life. But since Michael wanted me to go meet a ninety-one-year-old Trappist monk who'd been counseling combat veterans since World War II to talk about moral injury, I sort of had to go.

33

CONFESSION

I was squeezed into a packed car as it ambled along a mile-long dirt road that ended at St. Benedict's Monastery in Snowmass, Colorado. In it were me, Michael, and the entire teaching staff of the meditation workshop, including Ken, James, and Kathy, who cooked meals for the course participants every evening. The teachers didn't have to make the fifteen-mile journey to Snowmass — they just wanted to get up close and personal with the person we were going to see.

In the distance I could see St. Benedict's Monastery, a cluster of cream-brick buildings nestled in a valley beneath the twelve-thousand-foot twin summits of Mt. Sopris. As we drove closer, I noticed single-room hermitages that dotted the four-thousand-acre property, the structures dwarfed by the mountains above and the sweeping fields that surrounded the campus in 360 degrees.

Father Thomas Keating was a Trappist monk who'd first come to St. Benedict's in 1958. He was also one of the founders of the Centering Prayer Movement, a Christian meditation method first introduced to the modern world in the 1970s. Centering Prayer is similar to Buddhist meditation methods and teaches you to focus your mind on a single word or mantra during meditation. The practice became widespread after Father Thomas cowrote a book about it — though it wasn't yet called "centering prayer" — with some other Trappist monks at St. Joseph's Abbey in Massachusetts. Incredibly, James had first met Father Thomas at St. Joseph's many years before, when James was studying to become a priest. That day in Snowmass, James and Father Thomas were continuing a friendship that had lasted decades.

Since founding the Centering Prayer Movement and returning to Snowmass from Massachusetts, Father Thomas had become a world-renowned, beloved, and controversial figure in the Christian world. His ideas about the nature of religion, meditation, and God's love were published in dozens of books and translated into many languages. At talks around the world, Father Thomas appeared onstage with folks like the Dalai Lama. At St. Benedict's he hosted twelve meditation retreats a year, which drew people from all over the world.

And he'd agreed to spend his Thursday afternoon being interviewed for the documentary, and — gulp — talking to *me*.

I stood in the monastery's main library, which had been converted into a film set for the day. The film crew had tried to black out the tall windows so they could control the lighting, but some sunlight still managed to peek through and illuminate the staircase that spiraled between the tall bookshelves. Our group had been guided down a long hall that was filled with orchids and succulents, then past a chapel and into the cozy, carpeted library of unexpected books. I scanned the shelves looking for Bibles and books on Catholic doctrine. Instead, I saw titles on psychology, ancient philosophy, and modern physics.

Baffled by the collection, I planted myself in the corner, away from the camera crew and tungsten lights. We were all waiting for Father Thomas to arrive. I was growing sicker by the minute, my head pounding and my sinuses completely stopped up. I was also getting more and more nervous. The last time I talked to a priest one-on-one was during Catholic Confirmation class in high school. Confession, and practicing Catholicism in general, always made me feel shitty. In fact, feeling shitty about yourself seemed to be the point of the whole religion. You're born a sinner, you live as a sinner, and you'll die a sinner unless you confess your sins to a priest, aka God's middleman. As a teenager, the sins I had to confess seemed so despicable in the eyes of the priest, so foul, so condemnable, it wasn't the sin being condemned so much as me.

I masturbated.

I stole a book of matches from a convenience store.

I harbored impure thoughts about girls at school.

I remember pausing and waiting for the priest's thick judgment to waft through the gridded confessional screen and settle on my shoulders like a cloak. Technically, my punishment was reciting ten Hail Marys and fifteen Our Fathers, but the real punishment was the silent judgment the priest passed on me. My punishment was knowing that a holy man thought I was wretched to the core; I was a sick, twisted, masturbating thief unworthy of God's love.

And if I was that despicable because I jerked off or stole a matchbook, what was a priest going to say about the things I'd done during war? I had judged myself and condemned myself for the past ten years. I couldn't face the stern, tight-lipped judgment of a priest, too. Besides, I was pretty sure I could never say enough Hail Marys to make up for my time in Iraq. Once you move from masturbation and matchbooks to making war, you can't just say the rosary anymore.

By the time Father Thomas entered the library, I'd worked myself up into a miserable, and very congested, panic. I was hiding in the corner of the library because I wanted to disappear and hide from this priest's judging eyes.

Into the room, moving very, very slowly, stepped a smiling ninety-one-year-old man in an old fleece sweatshirt and new sneakers. He sat down in a chair, Michael rolled camera, and Father Thomas began answering Michael's questions. First Michael would interview Father Thomas. Then I'd join Father Thomas in the empty chair placed across from him, and Michael would ask both of us questions and guide the conversation between us.

While I waited to join Father Thomas, I listened to him speak. I could tell by the timbre of his voice and the light in his eyes that he wasn't there to condemn anyone. He wasn't even there to push a spiritual agenda on anyone. He was just there, in the room, fully present and fully awake to whatever the moment brought. His presence made everyone around him more present, too. The past disappeared. The future didn't matter. We all stood there, the teachers giddy and me completely amazed, just listening to him speak.

And then, for some reason, my brain shorted out.

Once Father Thomas sat down and started speaking, something happened that to this day I can't explain. The words that were coming out of his mouth suddenly seemed to be in another language. He seemed to stop speaking English and start speaking in some other language I couldn't understand. I tried to catch Michael's eye, but he was smiling and nodding and continuing to converse with Father Thomas. Michael was speaking English, and he seemed to understand this new, strange language Father Thomas was speaking. Was it Latin? Was Michael fluent in Latin and had just never mentioned it to me? I looked at James, then Ken, then Kathy and the rest of the film crew. Everyone was smiling and nodding as Father Thomas spoke. Everyone understood him perfectly well. Later, when I watched the interview on film, I could understand everything he said perfectly fine. I can only guess that at the time, he was saying something I wasn't ready to hear and that nature found a way to prevent me from learning something I wasn't quite ready for.

And then Michael was calling my name.

It was time to sit down across from Father Thomas.

I took a deep breath as best I could and emerged from my safe, warm cave behind the lights. I took my seat in the chair across from Father Thomas and allowed my eyes to meet his. When they did, I almost burst into tears.

Waves upon waves of kindness washed over me. Earlier I could see that there was no judgment in him. But now, sitting with him, I could feel it. He wasn't there to call me a sinner. He wasn't there to judge me — not even for the things I had seen and done in Iraq. He was there to listen to me, without judgment or agenda. He was just there to sit across from me and bear witness to my experiences. He wasn't waiting to offer a solution to a problem he hadn't yet heard. He wasn't gearing up to lecture me on how I'd failed myself and God. In Father Thomas, I sensed endless compassion for the darkest, sickest parts of the human heart, forgiveness for all without expectation or agenda. Complete forgiveness, which meant complete acceptance, which meant true, pure love. The love of nature. The love of God.

Maybe it was because of the new breathing technique we'd learned that day, but in Father Thomas's presence I felt more vulnerable than ever. And then it struck me, quite suddenly, that we shared the same first name. It took everything I had not to openly weep at his feet.

When he spoke, it once again sounded like English. It was as if those moments lost in translation had never happened.

Michael expertly guided us to the heart of his questioning, which was his great gift as a director. It's not easy to talk about moral injury with someone you've just met, but Michael and Father Thomas made it easier. If he'd asked for my confession, I would have given it to Father Thomas in a heartbeat. It would have been this:

Did you know that people like to think of us as heroes? Sometimes they'll say that. They'll talk about the heroic service of our brave men and women. And they'll mean our brave men and women in the military. Our brave men and women who have fought in wars.

I want you to know we got hit with a car bomb. I want you to know that I was in the air-guard hatch when it happened. I want you to know how exposed I was. How big that bomb was. Sometimes car bombs were small and pathetic, like someone stepping on a balloon. Sometimes they were like fireworks happening inside your head, and afterward, everything within a block radius would be on fire. This was that kind of bomb.

I want you to know that when the smoke cleared, I saw four guys hiding behind a car, peeking up at me. I want you to know that I locked and loaded. I want you to know it was a conditioned response. I want you to know that my only thought was to protect my friends. I want you to know I shot a hundred rounds into the car. I want you to know that I killed them all. I want you to know they were on the ground, and that we didn't stop to see if they were dead or alive, and that someone else had to peel them off the road and take them wherever you take the bodies of fathers and sons.

I want you to know that maybe they were the guys who set off the bomb. I want you to know that maybe they were just guys taking cover from the bomb. I want you to know that I'll never know.

I want you to know that I think heroes inspire people. They do good in the world. They save lives. They change lives for the better. They help people who are in distress. But that's not war. I want you to know that in war, no one is a hero.

But Father Thomas didn't ask for my confession. He seemed to understand without having to ask. I didn't have to say much to tell him everything.

"We have cadences in war," I confessed after some time. "They're like songs that talk about how 'we're gonna kill.' It's what we're there to do. So you do it. There isn't time to process it."

Father Thomas nodded. He seemed to consider what I'd said for a long moment.

"And so you're left with this raw, primitive feeling that you've done something terribly, terribly wrong," he said.

I nodded. We sat in silence again. No one else in the room

spoke or moved. All I could hear was my own labored breathing.

"You wonder if you were justified in doing the things you did," he continued, "and you don't know if you can be forgiven."

His words hit me like a ton of bricks. Somehow, in those two simple statements, he'd drilled down to the core of what moral injury really was for me: I didn't know if I could be forgiven. I didn't know if I *should* be forgiven.

"Antidepressants can't reach the depths of this pain," said Father Thomas. "But the human psyche has an enormous capacity to revive. If it only has a crack or a few moments of peace, it knows there is something beyond the immediate horrors it is seeing. That is what frees you."

All we need is the faintest glimmer of hope. That is enough to sustain us. That is enough to unleash the healing power that lies within.

Father Thomas looked straight at me.

"So there are only two questions that need to be answered. Can this man forgive himself? And can he forgive God for letting this happen?"

34

FORGIVENESS

I began the final day of the meditation workshop with a strange, unexpected intention: to forgive myself, and to forgive God. We were doing the new breathing technique again — long breaths followed by medium breaths followed by short breaths. James and Ken told us that no matter what happened, we were supposed to keep our eyes closed, keep breathing, and keep going. When you give a group of vets instructions like that, we do it, 100 percent. We were in it together. I felt ready to face whatever came up, whether it was flashbacks or indecipherable languages or anything else.

Later, I learned about these energy points in our bodies called chakras. These points exist at energy centers throughout the body, like the base of the spine and the top of the head. Our chakras can get clogged up with junk like trauma. Breathing and meditation can help loosen the junk and realign the body to its natural state.

We did the new breathing technique one final time. I didn't experience flashbacks this time, just some tingling and numbness in my hands and face. When we were done, we lay down to rest. It was then that I remembered the intention I'd set for that day's class. In a deep state of meditation, I recalled Father Thomas, his essence. I didn't quite recall his words, but I remembered the concept of forgiveness. I felt it like a question mark. Could I forgive myself for things I had and hadn't done in Iraq? Could I forgive God for the moral wounds that had nearly destroyed what was left of my life?

I didn't ask the question in my mind. I asked the question from somewhere deeper inside myself. I didn't need words or thoughts. This Q&A was between my soul and nature, or God.

A tingling sensation suddenly stirred at the base of my spine. It felt like something was opening up and unwinding itself from deep inside me. It was a physical sensation, but it wasn't just my physical body that was unraveling. I felt the sensation move upward along my spine. It gained momentum as it moved from my tailbone to the middle of my back, then up between my shoulder blades and into my throat. The sensation, the chakra, the whatever-it-was burst through my throat in a silent sob and came out as tears. There, lying on the mat surrounded by other veterans, I wept freely, and soundlessly, without sorrow or grief.

As I wept, a voice from within rose up and consumed me with the force of a rocket-propelled grenade:

You are forgiven, it said.

I felt the forgiveness permeate every cell.

And then, a response welled up from deep inside me.

I forgive you, too.

35

MORE THAN WOUNDS

A few days after the meditation workshop ended, I was back in Milwaukee, standing in the middle of the street, staring up at the sky. A thick sheet of clouds was moving slowly overhead, like gauze being pulled from a wound. Beneath that dim vault, a river of melting snow, dirty ice, and tiny tree branches rushed in a wet mess down the center of the street. Clumps of muddy grass — the sad remains of sloppy snowplows — were piled on the sides of the road. Trash from the whole winter dotted the landscape like a shameful secret exposed. And in that cold, wet, dreary spring scene, I stood beside my parked car with the driver's door open and my head tilted back, staring up at the drab, dark sky, thinking, "That is the most beautiful thing."

In that moment, the sky wasn't just beautiful *to me*; the sky truly *was beautiful*. In that moment, some sort of objective reality blossomed into existence, and the beauty of the sky wasn't an interpretation or an opinion; it was assured. I could see and feel it in my whole body. I was experiencing its beauty the way I might have experienced hunger or nausea or extreme fatigue or true love. When you're hungry or nauseous or exhausted or in love, you don't need to prove how you're feeling. You don't worry about whether or not other people believe in your experience. The experience itself is so acute and tangible that how it's perceived or interpreted doesn't matter a bit. You know it's true because you're living it. You're completely swept up in it and consumed by it. That's how it was the day I looked up and saw the sky for the first time in my life.

I also knew how *weird* it was to be standing there, in the wet street, staring up at the dark sky and thinking how beautiful it was. If there's one thing that unites all Wisconsinites, it's our collective disgust for the weather in late March and early April, when winter throws a temper tantrum as it finally cedes the stage to spring. In that moment, I was completely aware of how I'd *normally* feel when I looked at a sky so dark and drab. Somehow, my perspective had been completely reset. I didn't know why or how, but I knew that something fundamental had shifted inside me.

That fundamental shift wasn't just about the weather, either. During the course, they told us to stay away from meat and booze because we were detoxifying. Just like you wouldn't get wasted and eat rich foods during a cleanse, you weren't supposed to eat a bunch of garbage while doing intense breath work. I wanted to detoxify as much as I could, so I followed the instructions. For the past week, I hadn't had a drop of alcohol or so much as a chicken tender. And I felt great. Lighter, somehow.

When I finally tore myself away from the beauty of the sky, I went to see a friend. She'd cooked us a fancy steak dinner and had gotten a nice bottle of red wine. She'd gone to so much trouble, I couldn't bring myself to refuse. As soon as I finished the meal, I felt like a fever had come over me. My forehead pulsed as if someone was poking my skull from the inside. Not only did I feel physically sick, but the food and wine seemed to dull the strange sense of beauty I'd felt as I stood beneath the sky that day. It made the light, clear feelings I'd been feeling since the workshop disappear. And that sucked because I really, really liked those feelings. They felt much better than any food or drink or drug or medication had ever made me feel. As I sat there, stuffed with steak and wine, numb to beauty, and ready to hurl, I knew I was done with alcohol.

Meat took a little longer. During the course, it was easy to cut out meat altogether because vegetarian food was provided to us. Back home, I took it slow and cut down on meat over time. I stopped eating red meat first and ate turkey and chicken instead. Over the course of a few months, I started limiting meat to three times a week. On the other days, I'd try vegetarian recipes I'd never had before. It was a strange, new world. I wanted to make sure I was getting enough protein and that I was eating foods I actually liked. I was surprised at how easy it was for me. I was also surprised at how great I was starting to feel physically. It was like a weight was being lifted every single day.

But what surprised me the most was how much my diet impacted my meditation practice. Once I got back from the workshop, I really tried to keep up with the meditation and breath work. Ken and James had taught us breathing patterns we could do at home. I noticed that the less meat I ate, the deeper my meditations would be, and the longer I'd be able to sit without squirming. The less meat I ate, the easier it was to reconnect with my body. I learned that people who've experienced trauma tend to disassociate from their bodies. It becomes hard to tell when we're hungry or what our bodies really need. We may even use food to try to mute the feelings of trauma or numb the pain of moral injury.

Now it was much easier to tell which foods made me feel bad and which foods made me feel good. And so I found myself — a red-blooded Midwestern man raised on bratwurst and beer — starting to behave like a straight-up *sober vegetarian*. The shift felt strange in theory but natural in practice. It had nothing to do with ethics, or the environment, or politics, or any of the other commendable reasons a person might become a sober vegetarian. It was much more selfish than that.

I now had a choice: feel like crap or feel good. I wanted to keep feeling good. I wanted to keep feeling as good as I'd felt the day I looked up and saw the ugly sky as beautiful. I wanted to feel as good as I'd felt the day I'd wept tears of forgiveness in the workshop. I was willing to do anything or avoid anything to keep feeling that way. Besides cutting out alcohol and meat, the most powerful way to keep feeling that way was to keep meditating. Like, on the daily.

I sucked at meditation in the beginning. I'd do it for one day, then miss a whole week. Then I'd do it for three days but skip the fourth day. It went on like that for months. Meditation was really hard. It was hard to sit still. It was hard to do the breathing. It was hard to discipline myself to do it when I didn't feel like doing it. But I was determined to incorporate it into my life because when I stayed consistent with the practice, I felt like a completely different person.

And I wanted to share that feeling with other veterans. I started volunteering for the organization that had produced the workshop in Aspen. I worked with Ken, James, and Kathy to arrange meditation workshops for vets in Milwaukee. At the workshops we'd teach the same breathing techniques I'd learned in Aspen. We'd listen to the same tape I'd listened to. We'd do the patterned breathing technique — breathing slow, then medium, then fast. And I'd watch other vets have these incredible breakthroughs, just like I'd had. They'd feel like a weight had been lifted, just like me. They'd leave the course with a new sense of hope, just like me. Some of them would even start meditating regularly.

Even as I shared the breath work with more and more people, the process remained a mystery. How could something as simple as breathing be so powerful? How could breathing in a particular pattern release trauma so quickly and address moral injury so directly? How could it be that meditation, which was free and available to everyone, was the answer we'd all been searching for?

One day I got a call from James and Kathy, asking if I wanted to join the organization full-time. Not as a volunteer but as a full-time paid staff member. My job would be to travel around the country organizing meditation workshops for veterans.

By fall 2015 I found myself in Washington, DC, working for the organization full-time, living in a meditation center, and spending hours a day in meditation. Before I started meditating, I'd spent nearly ten years trying and failing to heal moral injury through every means I could find — talk therapy, drugs, alcohol, prescription medication, EMDR therapy, and a 2,700-mile walk across the country. Once I made meditation a part of my daily life, it took only eighteen *months* to reach a point I'd never dreamed of: not only was I not suicidal or depressed, but I no longer needed alcohol to numb the pain of moral injury. I could sit and be with myself for hours on end. I could even sit and think of the past without spiraling into sorrow. There was a distance between me and my past now. A buffer. Meditation didn't make the past disappear. It let me revisit memories without getting completely sucked into them. The past stayed in the past, and I stayed in the present.

I was traveling all over the country and sometimes abroad to do incredibly fulfilling work.

I was more than what I'd seen and done.

I was more than my wounds.

The future looked certain and bright. But the present moment, which I was learning to make friends with, looked even brighter.

36

MAN IN WHITE

The Sri Sri Center for Peace and Meditation was located in an old three-story building across from Meridian Hill Park in the Columbia Heights neighborhood of DC. Like many of the other buildings on the street, the meditation center was a converted embassy. When you entered, you'd slip past the sliding iron gates, cross a small courtyard, and climb the stairs to the main building lobby on the first floor. You'd look around for the urgent clip of embassy staff in their business casual blazers and uncomfortable shoes. And that's when you'd realize this place wasn't an embassy at all. Sure, there were chandeliers and parquet flooring with gold-and-cream-colored walls. But instead of folks in dark, muted clothing, you'd see people passing in saris with brilliant flashes of russet and blue. Instead of conference tables, you'd see meeting-room floors lined with purple and green yoga mats. Instead of microwavable Lean Cuisines, you'd smell the fragrant spices of Indian cooking.

The main meditation hall was on the second floor and was large enough to hold the dozens of people who came to practice meditation, yoga, and breath work. A smaller meditation hall was often filled with meditation students, teachers, and members of the public who were there to attend a lecture or class. On a typical day there might have been eight to ten people walking around the center. Some people lived there, like me. Others were there to teach a course or attend a meeting. On busy days, there could be up to fifty people there to take a meditation course or attend a program. There might be veterans learning breath work, or teachers training to conduct meditation courses in prisons or schools. The third floor of the meditation center was reserved for special visitors, including the founder of the organization, Sri Sri Ravi Shankar. He was the teacher who had developed the breathing techniques I'd learned in the workshop in Colorado. His organization was founded on the belief that all human beings are connected by a spiritual bond. This connective bond is stronger and more important than the things that separate us, like race, religion, and culture. He worked to promote core values of love, compassion, enthusiasm, and the creation of a stress-free, violence-free world. Sri Sri said that science and spirituality were complementary and inextricably linked to each other. He championed the breath as the link between the mind and body, and he believed that the breath could be used as a practical tool to reduce stress and relax the mind. Most important to me, he believed in being of service to others.

Sri Sri didn't push a religion or any particular dogma, which really appealed to me, too. I liked the focus on values and practical tools. His teachings promoted the importance of discipline, like meditating consistently, but there weren't hard-and-fast rules to follow. There wasn't a right or wrong side to be on, or the threat of hell for those who didn't make the cut. It was about trying your best, learning from your mistakes, and helping others do the same. Something about that felt right to me.

In fall 2015, just a few weeks after I'd moved to the meditation center, Sri Sri was scheduled to come to DC. My job was to coordinate a meeting between him and six veterans who had taken his meditation course. As far as logistics went, it seemed simple enough. Instead of having to travel to another city, recruit vets to take a course, facilitate the course itself, and organize everyone's travel, I could stay in town and take it easy. Travel for the vets had already been arranged. All I had to do was rent a van, pick up some guys from the airport, and make sure the group was sitting in the right room, at the right time, to meet with Sri Sri.

The day Sri Sri was scheduled to arrive, I came out of my room and saw a group of people sitting on the stairwell, scrubbing and polishing the wood floors, and wiping down the molding with wet rags.

"Looks like you're hard at work," I said to one of the women, who'd become a fast friend.

"Oh, this is nothing!" she said, beaming. "The last time he came, the vacuum was broken. I picked every piece of lint and dirt from the carpeting with my *fingers!*" she said.

I hesitated, unsure of how to respond. "Hmm," I said, finally, forcing a smile.

I tiptoed past her, sidestepping my way down the stairs so I could start my regular chores.

"Did they already pick him up from the airport?" someone asked.

"When's he going to get here?" asked another.

As I descended the stairs, I could feel a feverishness start to overtake the building. Dozens upon dozens of people were packed into the place, most of them Indian or Indian immigrants or the American children of Indian immigrants, all of them filled with a kind of joy and excitement the likes of which I'd never seen. My chores had long since been done by someone else. People started cleaning with an increased sense of urgency, maybe because someone texted someone that Sri Sri's flight had landed.

Some of the people at the meditation center considered Sri Sri their guru, or spiritual teacher. From what I could gather, this meant they believed in and followed his teachings, but also something more. Their devotion to him took on a spiritual significance for them. Being devoted to a guru gave a devotee a focal point outside themselves. It was a chance to practice gratitude, selflessness, service, and the acknowledgment of some sort of higher spiritual power. From my outside perspective, it seemed like the devotees thought Sri Sri was an enlightened master and they wanted to be more like him. I'd later learn that the most devoted of the devotees — maybe fifteen to twenty people — actually went to the airport to meet him after his plane landed whenever he came to DC. These folks were known as "guru chasers." Some of them spent epic amounts of time and money following Sri Sri around the world. When Sri Sri and his staff left the airport, the guru chasers would follow them across town in a caravan. With the snail's pace of DC traffic, the parade of cars may as well have been a presidential motorcade.

The crowd pushed its way through the center lobby, out the gates, and into the street. I stood in the lobby with my back against a wall, peering outside through a window overlooking the courtyard. I caught the eyes of my new friend, Jayshree, from across the room.

"C'mon!" she shouted, waving me toward her. "Come with me to greet him!" Her eyes shone brightly. It felt like everyone was waiting for a rock star to show up. I knew a lot of these people considered him their guru and everything, but did his devotees actually think this guy was a *god*?

"No thanks!" I shouted to Jayshree over the noise of the crowd. "I'm good!"

"Okay!" she said, smiling brightly. I watched her push her way through the crowd to the foot of a staircase and plant herself there on the first step. She knew the path Sri Sri would take as he crossed the lobby to his private quarters and was artfully positioning herself so he'd have to pass right by her when he climbed the stairs to his room.

Four or five cars pulled to a slow stop in front of the building. Doors opened, and half a dozen men got out of the cars. They were dressed all in white, in traditional kurtas that flowed to their knees. One of the men walked around to the passenger-side door of the first car. He opened it, and out stepped Sri Sri. I could barely get a glimpse of him because he was immediately swallowed up by the crowd. People waved and shouted and threw flowers. They gripped notes and gifts and tried to press them into Sri Sri's hands. Grown men and women wept openly at his feet, tugging at his kurta.

I suddenly wanted to get out of there, but there was no way through the crowd. Ironically enough, I could only stand to *be* in a crowd without having a panic attack because of Sri Sri's meditation techniques. When I did the breathing daily, as a discipline and a habit, the effects soothed me throughout the day — even when I wasn't meditating.

For a split second the crowd parted and I caught sight of Sri Sri. Brown skin. Black beard. He was less than a hundred yards from me, dressed in a traditional white kurta, flashing a wide, bright smile from person to person. He must have been in his late fifties then, but something about his smile made him look much younger. He'd let his hair grow long but kept his thick, black mustache and beard neatly trimmed. His sloping, prominent nose stretched proudly past his mustache. In his long, white robes, with his long hair and beard, surrounded by a crowd of feverish devotees, he looked positively Christlike.

Sri Sri's followers looked at him and saw love and light. I looked at him and felt wonder and fear. Not just a philosophical fear of losing myself again — after all, how easy would it be to replace the addictions I'd overcome with an addiction to meditation? — but an animal fear, a primal fear, an immediate fear upon sight. Suddenly, all I could see was his brown skin, his long black beard, his kurta. Somewhere deep inside, on a level that didn't register consciously until several years later, I thought this spiritual guru looked a lot like the man who tried to kill me in Iraq. And then I noticed the brown skin and black beards of the men all around me. These devotees, these seekers of peace, looked to me like Iraqi insurgents.

37

NUTS

Sri Sri entered the lobby of the meditation center. A small group of devotees lit lamps filled with ghee, or clarified butter. Someone placed a red *tilaka* dot on Sri Sri's forehead to welcome him. He then ascended the stairs, past Jayshree's perch, to retire to his private rooms to rest, clean up, and meditate. While Sri Sri rested, his devotees crammed themselves onto the stairwell that led to the meditation hall on the second floor. I stood still in the lobby, pressed against the wall, as the feverish mass roared past me. The panic of my subconscious flashback began to subside.

Holy shit. Now what?

I could go back up to my room and get some work done. Or I could go meditate with the group. I had no idea what to do because I was super uncomfortable. In my experience up until that point, that kind of adulation was usually reserved for a huge celebrity, not a spiritual figure. If you're like me and grew up Catholic, or if you were raised in some kind of Protestant Christian tradition in America, greeting a priest or pastor that way would have been pretty unthinkable. It's natural to try to find a frame of reference when things are new and different. When you can't find one, it's easy to get uncomfortable or creeped out — especially when thinking about gurus and devotees. In the West much of our exposure to gurus in popular culture has been around scandals — gurus who've abused their followers and manipulated them for their own profit. But I have to be honest. Standing in the meditation center that day, with my back against the wall and the buzz of excited chatter spilling down the stairs from the meditation hall, I was only worried about one thing. I wasn't scared of trying something new and different. And it didn't concern me that a few bad apples had given gurus a bad rap in America. Most Catholics don't throw out Catholicism just because some priests are evil. I didn't think there was any weird stuff going on, but if I found out there was, I'd hightail it out of there (and take the meditation techniques with me).

The only thing I was worried about in that moment was the risk of blindly following an institution without thinking for myself. That's what I'd done when I'd joined the military. During combat it had been necessary to act without thinking. It had been crucial to follow orders in order to survive. But I didn't ever want to find myself in that kind of situation again. The meditation and breath work were working for me. I wanted the freedom to grow at my own pace and use the tools that helped me the most. I didn't want religion or rules. I didn't want to lose myself inside a group again. I didn't know if the devotees were critical thinkers who had decided to follow their guru after a lot of internal debate, or if they were just blindly following him because it was easier than thinking for themselves. But their motivations didn't matter. What mattered was continuing to heal myself without losing myself again.

I took a deep breath. Then another. Paying attention to my breath helped me get out of my head. It helped me connect with a part of myself that seemed more in tune with what was right and wrong for me. I'd been trying to listen to that inner voice more and more. Conscious breathing slowed the mind and helped me listen to what was really going on inside me. What I found that day, when I paused for a few moments to breathe, was an inner strength I could trust. I could trust myself not to lose myself again. I knew so much more about what was and wasn't right for me, and I could trust myself to question and challenge those things that didn't align with who I was, and who I wanted to be.

By the time I decided I *did* want to join the group meditation in the big hall, all the good seats were taken. If you've never hung out with a bunch of devotees for a group meditation with their guru, there are three important things to keep in mind. First, you can't fully understand the meaning of the phrase *standing room only* until you've entered a meditation hall where people are literally sitting on top of one another. I looked for a place to sit down, but there was none. My choices were to try to meditate standing up (not ideal) or to try to sit down. So I sat down as best I could by inserting myself into (and sort of on top of) a cluster of seated devotees.

Second, once you insert yourself into a cluster of devotees, it's really, really hard to get up again. And if you do manage to get up, your seat would definitely be taken the second you left. Shortly after Sri Sri arrived in the hall and began leading a group meditation, I realized how bad I had to pee. I was intertwined with the bodies around me like plaid on a flannel shirt. There was no escaping — not until the meditation was over. So I held it. And held it. And held it. When everyone else was taking deep breaths and slipping into a meditative state, I held my breath and tried to think dry thoughts.

Third, don't be surprised if there are snacks. After the meditation, Sri Sri started throwing packets of almonds and trail mix into the crowd like a pop star shooting a T-shirt gun during a concert. I learned that this practice was part of the Hindu tradition of *Prasad*, where food is blessed and consumed after a ceremony or meditation session. It was a lot like Holy Communion in Catholicism, if the priest tossed out communal wafers like frisbees.

As I tried to untangle myself and make a beeline for the bathroom, Sri Sri threw a package of almonds straight at me. I reached out to grab them, but someone else snatched the nuts away midair. I looked back toward Sri Sri, who was staring right at me, smiling. He palmed another package of almonds and threw it at me again. I felt panicked — it's hard enough to catch a tiny package of nuts from across a large room, but now everyone was watching to see if I could do it. This time, my hand seemed to come to life of its own accord. Without any effort on my part, my hand seemed to raise itself up. The package of almonds flew straight into my palm, and my fingers closed effortlessly around it.

That was kind of bizarre, I thought as I practically leapt from the room, *Prasad* in hand, and skidded into the nearest bathroom.

After Sri Sri finished tossing out nuts, he was escorted by his entourage back up to the third floor of the meditation center. This was where he stayed when he was in DC, but it was also where he took his meetings. The entrance to the third-floor hallway was past a guarded staircase, where a guard would either deny you access or let you pass, depending on who you were and if you had an appointment. The door to the hallway at the top of the staircase was locked, so once you were okayed by the guard, you had to wait for someone to unlock the door from the inside. Later, I'd learn that it was important for the flow of visitors entering Sri Sri's room to be regulated so he didn't get bombarded all at once and so that all visitors were formally announced before entering his room.

I was standing on the second floor outside the meditation hall when James, my former meditation teacher and current boss, appeared by my side.

"I want you to meet Gurudev," he said, calling Sri Sri by the name many of his devotees called him. It meant something like "He who always remains a teacher."

"Cool," I said.

I followed James up the staircase to the door that led to the third floor.

"He's with me," James told the guard.

A few moments later, the door was opened from the inside and James and I were ushered into the hallway outside Sri Sri's door. Inside the hallway, security was pretty lax. None of the rooms were locked — not even the door to Sri Sri's meeting room.

"Wait here," said James. His voice sounded calm, but the look in his eyes said, "Wait here upon pain of death and do *not* even *think* about entering this room without me coming to get you first."

I sat on the floor in the hallway outside Sri Sri's room, waiting for James to come get me and bring me in. After a few minutes, the hall guard let a devotee enter the hallway. She was a white American woman dressed in a sari with a comfortable air that made me think she'd done this before. The woman strode right over to me and peered at me, cocking her head to one side.

"Aren't you going in?" she asked.

"Um…" I said.

"Come on, let's go in!" she said, gesturing toward the door.

"Well…" I said.

The woman smiled, turned, and grabbed the door handle to open it.

"Okay," I said, scrambling to my feet. "Let's go."

She pushed the door open and we walked into the room together.

The first thing I saw was Sri Sri's smiling face turn toward mine.

The second thing I saw was James's horrified face turn toward mine. His eyes bulged, his lips parted. I stood there, frozen, while the woman waltzed into the room and joined a dozen other people who were sitting on the floor before their guru. Sri Sri was sitting cross-legged on a love seat and surrounded by food and gifts. He looked like a child lounging in a giant pile of presents on Christmas morning. James held his death stare and slowly, silently tapped the empty chair next to him.

Late-autumn light spilled into the room from the windows that lined the far wall. There were plenty of chairs, but no one else sat in them. Sri Sri waved to me, then turned his attention back to the people sitting on the floor. Among them was a handful of children who were darting between him and the small crowd.

"Ooh, that's nice," he'd say when one of the kids stopped to show him a toy or trinket in their hand. Then he'd continue handing out gifts and treats to the people sitting on the floor.

"I told you to wait," hissed James in my ear. "Sri Sri likes to know who's coming in the room before they come in," he said.

"Oh, right. Sorry," I said, taking a seat in the chair beside him. The people sitting on the floor were lit up like lanterns. They were smiling and giggling, completely mesmerized by their guru. I knew his devotees thought Sri Sri was "enlightened," but I didn't really know what that meant. Did it mean he had magical powers? Could he read your mind? To me Sri Sri just seemed like a happy little person who was a good teacher. He dropped a lot of knowledge on his devotees and dropped a lot of money on charitable causes. But it was clear the people sitting on the floor — and choking the hallways and courtyards and meeting rooms — felt something more.

Sri Sri stopped taking visitors shortly after I entered the room.

"Okaaaaaay," he said suddenly, standing up from his couch.

And that was *all* he said, but everyone stood up and started filing out of the room. A few people tried to ask him questions before they left. That's when James pulled me by the arm and steered me toward Sri Sri.

"Gurudev," James said. "This is Tom Voss, the veteran we just hired to help us with the veteran outreach program."

"Hey, it's nice to meet you," I said, extending my hand for a handshake.

Sri Sri looked at me, threw his arms up, and wrapped them around me in a huge hug. He embraced me firmly, then released me and stepped back, looking straight at me.

"Are you happy?" he asked.

I opened my mouth to answer, but no words came out.

The next day, I led a group of six combat veterans, including Anthony, through the crowded meditation center, up the stairs, past the guard, into the hallway, and through the door of Sri Sri's room. The six of us sat in chairs that had been set up in a semicircle in front of his couch. We'd brought the veterans to meet Sri Sri so they could share their transformative experiences with him, including how their lives had changed after doing his breathing techniques. The group had twenty minutes to ask Sri Sri anything.

James ushered Sri Sri into the room. The guru looked much like he had the day before, outfitted in a long kurta with colored piping and a flowing shawl to match his robes.

"These are graduates of your program," said James.

Sri Sri started passing out *Prasad* to all the vets, who took the treats and held them over napkins, brushing tiny crumbs off their freshly ironed slacks and button-down shirts. Anthony, in shorts and a T-shirt, sucked a fat wad of chewing tobacco in his cheek, as was his ritual at speaking engagements and other important events like this one.

"Thank you so much for these breathing techniques," said one vet.

"Yeah, we're really grateful for your techniques," said another.

"These are not my techniques," said Sri Sri. "These techniques are for everyone," he said.

And with that, he let his gaze drift over the group. He looked at Anthony, then shifted his eyes from vet to vet until he landed on me.

He stopped and stared. I looked back at him, wondering why he was looking at me and what I should do about it.

Then he closed one eye and gave me this laser-blast stare through the other. He sat there staring at me through one open eye for what felt like forever, but it must have been three or four seconds. Then he opened his eye and continued gazing at the rest of the group.

What the hell was that? I wondered.

Did anyone else see that?

I stole a sideways glance at Anthony and the rest of the vets, but no one else seemed to have noticed the one-eyed-pirate stare the guy just gave me. *What was he doing?* I wondered. *Staring into my soul?*

Even though we had a chance to ask Sri Sri anything — a chance many of his devotees downstairs would've given anything to have — no one really knew what to ask, except Anthony.

"How could you come to a city like DC, where there's so much corruption and hate?" asked Anthony.

Sri Sri smiled at Anthony.

"That's exactly why we need to be here," he said.

The meeting was over. The veterans thanked Sri Sri again, and there was a lot of chattering and shuffling of chairs as we got up to leave. James and I were talking about the logistics of getting some of the vets back to the airport, I was fielding questions, and the whole group began moving toward the door.

Suddenly Sri Sri appeared next to me, seemingly out of nowhere. He glanced at me sideways, then let his gaze fall on the vets who were leaving the room. Very quietly, almost casually, he said, "You should come to India sometime."

38

BLISSED-OUT

When you get your head shaved in basic training, you go to a barbershop inside an AAFES store — Army and Airforce Exchange Service, like a military Walmart — and stand in line with fifty or sixty other guys. You stand silently, in parade rest, with your feet spread apart and your hands behind your back. You watch as groups of new recruits take their seats in barber chairs, get sheared like sheep, and then stand to make room for the next group of six. When it's your turn, you sit in the chair and look at yourself in the mirror. Your hair isn't that long. This should be easy. In the mirror, you glance sideways at the guy next to you. Under the buzz of the clippers, his shoulder-length hair is suddenly on the floor, dramatically splayed like bodies dropped from the sky. You look away.

You feel the pressure of the unshielded clippers, the blade grinding against your scalp. It's rough and over fast. There you are in the mirror — completely bald. You stand up and fall into formation alongside dozens of other bald heads. Any one of those heads may as well be yours. When you get your head shaved in basic training, you disappear.

When you get your head shaved in India, you do it in a field behind the meditation hall. You see a few guys standing in the tall grass beside plastic chairs. You pick one of the chairs and sit down. That's when you notice the bucket of water. You wonder what it's for. The guy beside the chair starts cupping water into his hand and sloshing it over your head. That's when you notice the straight razor.

You don't feel the pain at first. You just see the wide eyes of your friend, Rudra, who's standing in line to get his head shaved, too. You hear an angry exchange in Hindi, which is Rudra yelling at the man to take it easy, and the man telling Rudra to go to hell.

Slice, slice, slice.

Oh. *Now* you feel the pain.

Your hair falls freely to the ground. And maybe a few thin strands of your scalp do, too.

The man is supposed to save your hair and put the strands into a nearby river. When your hair is released into moving water, it's like letting go of your old self and being born anew. This simulated death and rebirth mark a new period of life when you'll follow a spiritual path, learn from a spiritual teacher, choose to live more simply, and basically meditate your ass off.

But the man just lets your hair fall into the grass, so Rudra yells at him again.

"Are you going to pick up his hair, strand by strand, and put it in the river?" yells Rudra.

The man yells back in Hindi. You don't understand what he's saying, but you wouldn't be surprised if "go to hell" has escalated to a more colorful set of curse words.

More friends arrive and stand in line to get their heads shaved. You see them exit the meditation hall, squint into the sun, spot you and Rudra, and make their way toward you. You see their jaws drop as they notice the bright-red lacerations across your scalp and the nicked facial skin where your long beard used to be. You are a bald, bloody baby now, except for the tiny rattail the man has inexplicably left unshaved at the base of your skull. Later, you'll hear that the rattail symbolizes an anchor that keeps you grounded to the earth. Most of your hair has disappeared into the tall grass instead of into a river, and your naked flesh is directly exposed to the harsh elements of India — the morning heat, the incessant flies, and the scent of burning garbage that fills the air.

"Dude. You look like you just got in a fistfight," says Rudra.

When you get your head shaved in India, you appear. Broken and bloodied and ridiculous, but you're seen — even though the people who see you are slightly horrified at the sight of you. You're not afraid of losing yourself anymore, of being coerced by groupthink, or of disappearing. Your mind and body are your own. You have agency. You are responsible for yourself. The past is still there, but instead of scratching its nails down your back and hijacking the present moment, it's sitting in a corner, behaving itself. And when the past behaves itself, there's nothing to fear in the present moment. You're alive. You're in the world. You're part of things in a way that makes sense to you. You might have a serious skin infection to deal with, but damned if you're not there.

I was somewhere outside the city of Bangalore, India, sitting on a mat in an enormous outdoor meditation hall, while a family of fifteen or so monkeys jumped from rafter to rafter above my head. The people who ran the meditation hall told us that whatever we did, we should *not mess* with the monkeys. There were babies and females and juveniles who'd swing down from the rafters and plop onto the ground in front of us. Sometimes an innocent person who didn't know any better would approach the monkeys on the ground and try to pet or feed them. I'd watch the sole male monkey stalking them from the rafters above, getting closer and closer, ready to pounce. Rudra sat beside me on the side of the hall reserved for men. I could see more friends and familiar faces from DC on the side reserved for women. We were all there to participate in an *upanayana* ceremony — an ancient ritual that marks the beginning of a student's formal study with a teacher. Sometimes called the "sacred thread ceremony," *upanayana* involves receiving a thread that you wear across your chest. This sacred thread represents your commitment to spiritual study and a spiritual path. It also represents your commitment to responsibility — to yourself, to your family, and to your community. After the ceremony, you're considered a *brahmacharya* — a spiritual student who pursues a simple, virtuous lifestyle that includes meditation and study.

If you want to become a *brahmacharya* in India, you've gotta wear a skirt. I was wrapped up like a birthday present, wearing a traditional dhoti, a fifteen-foot swath of shiny yellow cloth that Rudra helped me wrangle. Yellow is meant to symbolize spiritual abundance and wealth. The dhoti had to be wound around my waist and legs, tossed over and around my shoulders, and knotted at the waist. The fabric gathered in little piles around my neck like a turtleneck, then draped across my front like a giant cloth napkin. It was definitely not an outfit I'd ever imagined myself wearing, but in the Bangalore heat, it was highly breathable — sort of like a Snuggie, but for summer.

The ceremony began. I was given my sacred thread, or *yajnopavita*. Like my dhoti, the thread was yellow. It had been rubbed in turmeric and would eventually fade to white. The larger thread was actually made of three individual threads, each with different meanings. The first thread represented my responsibility to my family. The second represented my responsibility to my community. The third represented my responsibility to knowledge — to seeking spiritual knowledge, using it properly, and respecting it. The larger thread was placed over my head and under one arm, so it laid sideways across my chest, from my left shoulder to my right hip. Historically, the right hand was considered the strong or dominant hand. It was the hand you used to do important things. The right side of the body was associated with strength. So the sacred thread was worn over the *left* shoulder to signify that these responsibilities weren't a burden to me — I didn't even need to use my strong side. These responsibilities were easy and light; I welcomed them and fulfilled them with ease and gratitude.

Once a year, I'd retire the string by returning it to nature. Maybe I'd place it on a tree branch or bury it beneath a bed of flowers. Then I'd undergo another sacred thread ceremony to renew my commitment to spiritual responsibility. I'd get a new sacred thread and place it across my chest, fortifying my spirit for the year ahead. At the end of my life, when my responsibilities to family and work and myself had been fulfilled, and when I could no longer sit for hours in meditation, I would retire my last sacred thread. I'd immerse it in a rushing river or release it from the top of a mountain. And with that release would be the release of my spirit back to nature. Back to God.

I closed my eyes. The shawl from my dhoti was placed over my head so I couldn't see anything. We waited while the teachers performing the ceremony went through some rituals we couldn't watch. I don't know what they did or what took place. Then a swami, or master teacher, came around to each initiate to whisper the Gayatri Mantra to us, and I heard sacred words being whispered into my ear. Like the sacred thread, head shaving, and ceremony, the Gayatri Mantra was another traditional part of the *upanayana* ritual. It's a blessing with many meanings that vary depending on who's interpreting, but a loose interpretation could be: *We meditate on God, the Creator, whose divine light illuminates everything in existence. May this divine light illuminate our body, mind, spirit, and intellect.*

After the swami whispered the mantra into my ear, I felt a thick, heavy garland of flowers being placed over my head and onto my shoulders. Jasmine, hibiscus, marigold. It felt like a fat, fragrant boa constrictor had coiled itself around me. The weight of the packed petals made me feel grounded and safe. Next to me Rudra was weeping. He had waited his whole life to take part in this ritual and was swept away with gratitude, the front of his yellow dhoti stained with tears.

During the rest of the *upanayana* ceremony, I made offerings of rice to the divine and learned a sacred ceremony, *Sandhyavandanam*, that I could perform three times a day once I got back to the States. The ceremony involved meditation, but it also involved chanting. Chanting was a lot like saying the rosary in Catholicism. You repeated the same words over and over again. It gave your mind something to do so it was easier to slip into a meditative state. The words we chanted were pretty sacred, too — some of the prayers were thousands of years old. Chanting was new and a bit foreign to me, but meditation had been working so well that I figured I may as well try it; the more methods I had to heal from moral injury the better. And if chanting made me feel half as good as meditating did, I was more than ready to add it to my daily routine. For me, the most freeing part of participating in the ritual was that it was my choice. I could make these traditions a part of my life in whatever capacity I wanted to. It wasn't Hinduism; it wasn't even religion. I was given tools I could use to understand myself and the world. There was no punishment for not performing the rituals, no hell or purgatory to fear if I made a mistake. I didn't have to think like everyone else around me or agree with their beliefs. We were free to debate and disagree, and to agree and maintain our individuality. I was in control of my own spiritual destiny, with as much support or freedom as I needed.

At the end of the ceremony, as I returned to my seat on the ground beneath flying monkeys, wrapped in fifteen feet of shiny yellow cloth, sober and beginning to forget what pepperoni pizza tasted like, with my sacred thread binding the wounds of moral injury, holding me together beneath my dhoti, and the cuts on my scalp and face already beginning to heal, here is what taking part in *upanayana* meant to me:

Oh, nature
Oh, divine everything
Oh, giver and taker of life
Oh, bringer and destroyer of suffering
Oh, you who is everything and nothing and all things and
Everything in between
Fill me with your light
Awaken me to your love
Help me recognize the love and light
That burn and shine inside me, always
Purify and guide me along this path
Give me wisdom to listen
Connect me to you, to others, to myself
To all your creation
Even on days when I feel like shit.
Om. Shanti, Shanti, Shanti.

The mantra and the ceremony began and ended by chanting *om Shanti*. *Om* is the primordial sound, the beginning and the end, the great connector across all languages and religions and peoples and times. *Shanti* means "peace." The three vowel sounds that make up *om* are *A, U,* and *M*. These three sounds represent the three stages of universal creation. *Om,* or *A-U-M,* looks and sounds a lot like *amen*. And *amen* sounds pretty much the same in most languages. It's *amém* in Portuguese, *amin* in Serbian, and *ameni* in Chichewa/Nyanja. In Icelandic and

Lithuanian, Swedish and Vietnamese, Afrikaans and English, the meaning of *om* is expressed as *amen*. In Arabic, it's *'āmīn*. The prayer of the devout. The pleading of a grief-stricken parent in a war zone. The last words on the lips of an Iraqi child taken in the chaos.

I sat on the ground, bound and blessed, to appear and disappear into the endless *oms*.

And *om* became *'āmīn* became *om* became *'āmīn*.

And I was all the lives I had taken and lost. And I became all my brothers. And they were all there, and they were all me, and we were all free.

For ten days straight following the ceremony, I meditated and chanted from predawn until dusk. In the darkness, in my room at the ashram, I'd wake, roll out of bed, and sit on the floor. I'd do the breathing technique I learned from Sri Sri when I first listened to his voice on the tape during the meditation workshop in Colorado: slow breaths, medium breaths, fast breaths, repeat. Then I'd go and chant for hours at a time — at sunrise, at noon, and at sunset. After the sun went down, we'd all attend *satsang*, a sacred gathering, to sing *bhajans* — sacred songs.

Do you know what happens when you meditate and chant for hours on end for ten days straight? I'll tell you: you get blissed out of your mind. For ten days I walked around the grounds of the ashram feeling as high as a kite.

In that state of pure, waking bliss, the pain of the past had vanished completely. I felt comfortable in my own skin. I enjoyed meeting new people and being around others. I was perfectly comfortable being alone, too. I wasn't anxious about the future or depressed about the past. My thoughts slowed down.

I felt like a tree or an animal or a child — I just *was*. I was just there. I wasn't trying to do anything, make anything, or be anything in particular. That subtle ache of always wanting to be anywhere *except* where I was subsided and in some moments disappeared completely. A spotlight emanated from inside me; I was the source of the light.

I noticed that I wasn't trying to heal myself or contemplate moral injury or "feel more spiritual," whatever that meant. I wasn't thinking about religion. I wasn't even wondering if the ritual I'd just undergone meant I was Hindu now. No one mentioned anything about Hinduism, by the way. No one told me I had to read a certain book or follow a certain spiritual leader or swear off all the other religions for one particular religion. There was none of that, and I wanted none of that. I didn't want things to be any different from how they were. For the first time in my life, I accepted life for what it was and people for who they were. That meant I could accept myself for who I was, too, including my past — including moral injury.

I dove deeper into the ancient traditions that surrounded me. Thousands of years of open-source knowledge were mine for the taking, and I opened myself to every idea, no matter how at odds with my beliefs at the time. I learned more about Shiva, an aspect of the divine that represented both infinity and destruction. Shiva had no beginning and no end but was also a fearsome warrior charged with destroying the universe at the end of time. How could a being that had no beginning or end be responsible for ending the world? How could an all-loving, infinite god of gods manifest as an unconquerable warrior? How could a warrior capable of destruction still have infinity within him and divine love permeating his every cell? And if Shiva could destroy and make war and still be made of divine love, did that mean I could be, too?

These stark contradictions were possible, I learned, because nature includes everything. The love of nature, or God, does not discriminate between the rain that falls on a field and the shower of bullets that falls on a vehicle during combat. God is in all things and of all things. God was there when my bullets flew from my weapon into the bodies of the men that I killed. God was there when I wanted to kill myself. There is nothing I can do to disconnect myself from God, for God is in all things, God *is* all things, *including* me. I am a part of that love, that divinity, that oneness with all time, whether I feel it or not, whether I realize it or not. I'm connected to that because I come from that. God was with me in war, God expressed itself as war, and God was in the pain and sorrow and suffering of the aftermath of war, too.

So I accept moral injury not as a curse or punishment but as my divine gift, my holy lesson, my karma to overcome through meditation.

Am I condoning war, or trying to justify some of the actions I took during combat?

No.

War is never a choice we should aspire to. I believe God is present during war, but I don't know why war happens. I don't know why any of the bad things that happen in our lives happen at all. But when they do, I know they're not somehow happening *outside* of nature or *apart* from God. And because of that, I know we can use these experiences as catalysts for growth, healing, and peace. Bad things have an inherent connection to God — like poison and its antidote, even the worst experience has embedded in it a connection to its opposite, its source for redemption. If we look hard enough, we can find meaning inside the pain, transform trauma into power, and make the suffering worth something. War isn't meaningless if it ends with you.

During my time in India, Sri Sri came home to his Bangalore ashram. The feverish scene that had happened in DC played out in much the same way in India, but bigger and louder, with even more people (and even more snacks). Sri Sri was famous and revered around the world, but he was particularly celebrated in India, his homeland. At his ashram in Bangalore, hundreds of devotees milled about the grounds, hoping for a face-to-face meeting with him. I watched Sri Sri's arrival at the ashram in the same way I had in DC — from the background. I watched the caravan of cars pull up, the men in the white kurtas get out, the passenger-side door open and Sri Sri emerge. I watched the crowd spring toward him, their arms outstretched, like over-joyed children reunited with their mother.

I signed up for a time to meet with Sri Sri while he was in Bangalore. Just like in DC, he had a dedicated meeting room where he'd sit and receive guests. But here the group of ten to twelve people sitting on the floor at his feet had nearly tripled. Each person was given a few minutes to speak with Sri Sri, give him a gift, or ask for his blessing.

When it was my turn to meet with my teacher — he was considered my teacher now, officially, since I'd gone through the ceremony — I entered the crowded room and looked for a place to sit.

Sri Sri was midconversation with someone else, but his eyes met mine when I entered the room. And then he waved at me.

Imagine you hadn't seen your best friend in five years. You're attending an event, like a concert or something, and the event is in a huge auditorium packed with people. You're looking for your seat, when suddenly you spot your friend in the crowd — you'd know them anywhere. As soon as you spot them, they turn and look straight into your eyes, even across the distance of the space. And their eyes light up with recognition and joy. They smile a huge smile as they wave to you. And in that smile and wave is all your shared history, every moment of your friendship, and every ounce of love that they feel for you. That's how it feels when you walk into a room and Sri Sri looks at you and waves.

I couldn't find a spot on the floor, so I just stood at the back of the room. I wasn't waiting for anything. I just stood there, breathing in and out, comfortable as can be, not thinking much of anything. Just smiling like a blissed-out fool, completely content and at home in myself.

After a few minutes, one of Sri Sri's staff approached me.

"It's your turn," he said. "Are you ready to go talk to him?"

"No, thanks," I said. "I'm fine."

"You don't have anything you want to ask him?" he asked.

"Nothing comes to mind," I said.

"Okay," shrugged the staff member, walking away.

There was nothing to say to Sri Sri. I imagined that anything I had to say, he somehow already knew, anyway. But mostly there was nothing to say because there wasn't anything I wanted. It seemed then that anything I needed to know would be revealed to me in time. I was sure that if I kept up with the discipline of meditation, and chanting, and the spiritual path I'd undertaken, I'd get exactly where I needed to go, when I needed to get there. To my absolute amazement, that didn't just mean numbing the pain of moral injury or planting small seeds of hope for a future that was different from the present. I had moved beyond neutralizing pain, letting go of the past, and hoping for the future. I was tapped into a part of myself that I believe is also a part of you and everyone else who's ever lived or will ever live. It's divine love, or consciousness, or whatever word you want to use that means "peace." It is deep, timeless, and absolute. It feels fleeting, because we experience it only fleetingly. But it's always there. Tapping into it through meditation or chanting or exercise or nature reminds us of who we really are. And maybe someday, if we're really disciplined and really present, those experiences of blissful peace will grow longer and longer, and maybe even become our new normal.

One time, when Beck was traveling in Laos, she went to a Buddhist temple to meditate with the monks who lived there. After the group meditation, there was a Q&A session. Beck's question to the monks was, "I've had these incredible, transcendental experiences during meditation where I experienced myself as a point of pure consciousness. It even felt like I left my body, or like I had no body at all. But it only happened twice, and it hasn't happened since — probably because I *want* it to happen, and the act of wanting seems antithetical to that state of pure being, where I had no desires or thoughts at all. What can I do to have those experiences again?"

The monks didn't speak English well enough to answer, so this Indian guy in the audience answered on their behalf.

"Meditation isn't about *experiences*," he said. "You shouldn't be doing it because you're trying to have a particular experience."

"But what if the experience you had made you feel closer to God?" asked Beck.

"It's not about experience. It's about discipline and devotion. That is your reward for practicing meditation. If you *happen* to have a fulfilling experience, that's icing on the proverbial cake," he said. "But it shouldn't be your main motivation."

I disagree. If you're chasing cool experiences and that motivates you to keep meditating, go for it. Chase those experiences. Just the possibility of experiencing divine consciousness, in all its inexplicable wonder, could be enough motivation to keep you meditating for the rest of your life. I can't guarantee you'll have an out-of-body experience while you're meditating. I can't guarantee you'll have an experience that's so real it makes faith unnecessary. Meditation might not work that way for you. But if you keep up with it, I'd bet my left foot that at the very least, you'll feel better than you do right now. And you'll *keep* feeling better and better the longer you stick with it. It's the practice of sticking with it — along with the experiences you have because you've stuck with it — that heals you, and heals you, and keeps healing you, forever.

I was standing in the biggest outdoor arena I had ever seen. It was three football fields long and packed with millions of people. My trip to India had coincided with World Culture Festival, a three-day event celebrating cultural plurality, diversity, and acceptance. It was held on a seven-acre stage, where thirty-seven thousand artists, musicians, and performers from

155 countries shared their talents with the world. The festival marked the thirty-fifth anniversary of one of Sri Sri's foundations and was produced entirely by volunteers. I was pretty sure you could see the stage from space.

Since my time in Iraq, standing in a crowd had always given me panic attacks. Maybe that was because Mosul was such a crowded city. Or maybe I just hated being around people because I hated myself and was reflecting that hatred outward. Back home I'd feel repulsed when I looked at faces in a crowd or heard the stupid things people would say. But at World Culture Festival, I was standing in a crowd that was almost twice as big as the entire population of Mosul at the time I was there, and I was beyond fine — I was overjoyed.

I was a speck in the crowd, which seemed to move and undulate as a single organism. Michael Collins was there and someone tried to pick his pocket. Gabriel was there and actually got his phone, wallet, and passport stolen. Rudra was there, his bald head scraped up like mine. We were perfect imperfections, so sadly and beautifully human, victims of each other and champions of each other; a huge, dysfunctional, functional family. People danced and shouted, laughed and prayed, meditated and sang. The Argentinians were the absolute wildest — they'd sing and dance and cheer and laugh! We all chugged bottled water and sucked down chai tea shooters and pissed where we weren't supposed to. The pickpockets and sinners danced with the saints and became them. Together, we all roared with ecstasy when Sri Sri took the stage.

As millions of us sat and meditated together, following the sweet, soft timbre of Sri Sri's voice, I slipped once more into that natural state: I felt connected to everyone who'd attended the festival over the past three days: all 3.5 million of them. And from that connection, I came to love each and every one of them. And as I loved them, I became them. And as I became them, we all became one. It was then that I finally understood the difference between groupthink and true connection, true oneness. In groupthink, a group of people share the same mind — a small mind, a cerebral mind, a mind that is afraid and needs to protect itself and strengthen itself by joining up with other small minds. But true connection, true oneness with others, happens on a different level. True oneness happens when individuals tap into the big mind; it is not brain to brain, but soul to soul. It is the place where we connect with each other and with those whose bodies and small minds have passed on. It's the place where Clark and Diaz and all those we lost are found again, and free.

As I meditated in the stadium, the parts of me that were Tom remained intact. My small mind remained my own. But the part of me that had been wounded, the part of me that was still healing, reached out to everyone around me and connected, big mind to big mind, soul to soul. And then I tapped into some sort of oneness, one big mind, one soul. As part of that soul, I became nothing — the constructs of my small mind fell away, and I identified as nothing but pure consciousness. The nothingness of that moment was everything. I was lost in eternity, and so I was forever found. From that place of nowhere and nothing, where I was removed from my body and my small mind and my past, the me that was pure consciousness was able to observe the me that was Tom. I loved that guy so much. I felt such compassion for him, for his past, for his pain. I even forgave him, once again, just for good measure.

When the meditation ended, I was Tom again, back in my body, tapped into my small mind with acute awareness of the big mind. I was back in the beautiful world, writhing with gratitude. It was all I could do not to kick up my legs and do a goddamn cartwheel.

I was at peace. I was forgiven. I was free.

39

LUNCH BREAK

On your lunch break back in DC, you cross the street to the park and walk south along Fifteenth toward U Street, past people your age in pressed suits and pencil skirts. You watch their tense faces as they shout into their phones or sigh impatiently at crosswalks, their headphones blaring. A young man in a blue blazer stops in front of a bar with darkened windows, scowls at his phone, and takes off down the street. His fast pace reminds you to slow down. You continue south, sauntering down Fourteenth Street, where men shake each other's hands too firmly and women strut in Ann Taylor cotton-stretch twill. You notice the smiles that are plastered across their made-up faces and the perfect postures they strive for, their shoulders rolled forcefully down their backs.

You have no master's degree, no high-powered job to covet, no influential connections. You are invisible in Washington, except to the veterans you're helping. To them, you are the guy asking them to do something they'd never thought of doing — participate in a free meditation workshop. At first most of them just say no. Meditation? What for? They're not into that woo-woo health stuff; that's for hippies and vegans. But after nearly a year, you've figured out the trick. You know how to get veterans to do something that scares them — by showing them how it'll help someone else.

"Would you like to participate in the workshop?" you'd ask. "The other vets who'll be there could really use your support."

It was true. And it was equally true that the vet you were inviting to participate needed to be there for him- or herself; it was just easier to frame it as service to someone else. Maybe that makes this work easier for you, too. To think of it not as healing yourself, which it is, but as helping others. Either way, you know it's a blessing and an honor.

At Amsterdam Falafelshop, you order at the counter. Bob Marley music pulses a few decibels too loud. While you wait for your lunch, you eye the European decor and art deco wallpaper, distracting yourself from having to pick a place to sit. Then your sandwich is ready. It's placed on a tray piled high with too many french fries. You work your way through the toppings bar, choosing yogurt and hummus, beets and red cabbage. You skip the pickled cauliflower but slather on the jalapeño cilantro paste, your favorite. It's all vegetarian. And then it's time. You have to choose somewhere to sit.

The counter along the front windows has a nice view of the door and the street beyond. It's the perfect spot for a vet with

PTSD who needs to know who's coming and going from the restaurant at all times — someone who can't sit with his back to the door.

You choose a table in the center of the room, away from the counter. Then you sit with your back to the door, just to see how it feels. Just to see if, after eleven years of not being able to do it, you can.

The door opens, and you hear two people come in. Your pulse quickens ever so slightly, but you don't move. You don't turn to see who they are. You do not assume they are carrying weapons or wearing bombs. In fact, the thought does not even cross your mind. Their conversation floats above you briefly as they join the growing line. So-and-so left this firm to join that firm. You smile, relieved.

You bite into your sandwich, crunching through the thick, savory falafel crust, letting the jalapeño paste coat your tongue. You glance again at the various paraphernalia around the room — framed illustrations of little Dutch boys and girls; postcards from Amsterdam; a photograph of a topless young woman in a black skirt and black boots. She is presumably Dutch, presumably a lady of the night or of the past. You don't think about the past. You don't think about the future. You don't wonder what all the art on the walls means, or if your life has meaning. You sit alone and eat your lunch. You taste every bite. You know that even though you're eating lunch alone, you can never truly be alone because you're connected to everyone, always — the woman pictured on the wall, the people in the restaurant, the people rushing around DC, the people sitting *satsang* on the other side of the world in Bangalore. Even the people whose bodies are gone, the people who are part of the big mind forever. Those you lost are gone but not destroyed. Next to the women on the wall, you notice a handwritten sign that's been placed on top of a framed display case. The sign reads Make Falafel, Not War.

"Jai gurudev," you think.

AFTERWORD

I thought I was writing this book because I wanted to give you a glimmer of hope. My goal, when I started out, was to help you find some relief from pain. But you deserve more than that. You can have so much more than that. You *are* so much more than that.

You may feel 100 percent certain that you'll never feel any better than you do right now. You may want to crawl right out of your skin because the past is crushing you and it hurts so damn much to be *you* every day.

I know how much it hurts. I know how fucking unbearable it can seem.

But God is in the pain.

God is everywhere. God made everything and *is* everything. So God is in your pain, too.

But pain is not the ultimate truth. Pain is an illusion of this world. It's not who you really are in the grand scheme of things. In our world, God manifests as good and evil, the truth and the lie, the light and the darkness. But your true nature is much bigger than what happens here.

You don't have to believe that God is in everything and that everything happens for a reason. You don't have to see moral injury as a gift, a powerful teaching tool that's meant to forcibly, painfully, remind you who you really are. You don't have to believe that the shitty things that happen to us are our best learning opportunities meant to shake us and wake us up and change us for the better. You don't have to understand that moral injury highlights who you *aren't* — that the pain and grief and guilt and shame hurt so much because those things are so contrary to your true nature. You don't have to understand that it hurts to experience moral injury because moral injury is *so not you.*

But if you take one thing away from my story, I hope it's this: even when you feel consumed by moral injury and alone in the world, you are not separate from the beauty and good that exist here. You are still a part of that. You are connected to that, whether you feel it right now or not. You can experience that beauty and goodness again, if you want to.

If you cry out for help and relief, help and relief will come. They may come as a man painted in black and white, with feathers and a dead wolf on his head. They may come as a quiet, kind, mustached man or a herd of deer at the window. Help and relief might come as a kindly teacher, but they may come as a small, brown-eyed boy begging you for a piece of candy, or a girl who dies in the arms of your friend. They may even come as a man in black diving behind a parked car as he tries to end your life.

Healing begins when you stop resisting the teachers in your life, no matter their form, and start getting curious. Get curious about your pain. Start asking questions about it — about where it comes from, what's causing it, and what might make you feel better. Then get curious about the ways in which you're trying to heal. You might ask questions like, "Why am I always in such a shitty mood after I drink?" or "Why do I still feel depressed even though I'm on medication?" If you ask questions and seek truth with an honest heart, the answers will appear. In the meantime, a good place to start is right where you are. So sit down, get still, and take a deep breath. Then maybe take another. If it's hard to sit still, ask why. If you feel lots of resistance, get curious about that. Be gentle with yourself. Setbacks are okay. Setbacks will happen. If you're still breathing, there's more right with you than wrong. If you're still breathing, there is hope.

ACKNOWLEDGMENTS

We are deeply grateful to the many people who contributed to this book. Huge thanks to Emma Seppälä for making the connection that got this project off the ground. To our agent, Giles Anderson: Thank you for taking a chance on us. You believed in us, so we believed in us. Jerry Greenwald: Your continued support has made projects like this possible. Thank you for your generosity and faith in the mission. Thomas F. Swanson: Thank you for telling us where the story began.

To the incredible team at New World Library, where to even begin? Georgia Hughes: You gave us a resounding "Yes!" when we had grown accustomed to "Yes! But no!" Thank you for believing in the importance of this story. Jason Gardner: Your editorial genius lies not only in your light touch and tireless positivity, but in your ability to shepherd newbies like us through the creative process. Thank you for making it easy, cringing in all the right places, and knowing exactly when we needed to be trusted or pushed. It has been a joy and an honor to be guided by you. Mimi Kusch: You helped us think bigger so this story could reach a wider audience — thank you. Monique Muhlenkamp, Munro Magruder, and Ami Parkerson: Thank you for getting this book out into the world so it can help as many people as possible. Tracy Cunningham, Kristen Cashman, Tona Pearce Myers, Tanya Fox, and the rest of our New World team: Thank you for your enthusiasm, artistry, and ideas, big and small — each one has helped make this story what it is.

Anthony Anderson: Endless thanks for your memory, documentation, and willingness to let us dive deep into a story and time that belong to you as much as Tom. Michael Collins, WolfWalker, Jim Warren, Emmet Cullen, Gideon De Villiers, Clarissa De Los Reyes, and the Ulanski family: This story would not be the same told without you — not in this book, and not in Tom's life. Special thanks to Michael for your astonishing generosity in allowing us to share so many moments that have already been beautifully captured in your film *Almost Sunrise*.

To early draft readers and feedback givers: You have shaped this book from the beginning. Thank you, Rebecca Amrhein, JT Cardwell, Emmet Cullen, Dani DeVasto, Megan Gleason, Angela Pryor, Ryan Spiering, Indumathi Viswanathan, and everyone who told us what they *really* thought.

Debanti Sengupta: Thank you for your time, your expertise, and the sacrifices you made in giving us feedback. So much of this book works better, or works at all, because of you.

To our family and friends: Thank you for your many contributions to this accomplishment. We couldn't have done it without you: Patrick and Margie Voss; King, Patrick, and Aden Nguyen; Rebecca Amrhein; and Alexis McMorris.

To those who live on in the pages of this book and in Tom's heart — Mack, Solo, Zack, and Ian: You are free, but never forgotten.

RESOURCES

Art of Living Foundation:
https://www.artofliving.org/us-en

National Suicide Prevention Lifeline: 1-800-273-8255

Project Welcome Home Troops
Power Breath Meditation Workshop:
http://www.projectwelcomehometroops.org
/power-breath-workshop

Stop Soldier Suicide: https://stopsoldiersuicide.org

Vetoga: Yoga, Meditation, and Healing Arts:
http://vetoga.org

ABOUT THE AUTHORS

Tom Voss served on active duty in the United States Army for three years, from 2003 to 2006. Tom served with the 3rd Battalion, 21st Infantry Regiment, an element of the 1st Brigade, 25th Infantry Division, one of the army's first Stryker Infantry Brigades. He served as an infantry scout in the battalion scout-sniper platoon.

Tom is one of the subjects of the Emmy-nominated film *Almost Sunrise*, which documented his 2,700-mile trek from Milwaukee to Los Angeles.

For his work empowering veterans to overcome moral injury, Tom has been featured in the *New York Times*, *Newsweek*, *National Geographic Adventure*, *Men's Health*, *USA Today*, *Fox News*, the *Chicago Tribune*, *Epoch Times*, and the *Hollywood Reporter*. Tom has given presentations and lectures about his journey of hope and healing at Google, the Aspen Ideas Festival, New York University, the Medical College of Wisconsin, and the US Congress. He lives in Ojai, California.

Rebecca Anne Nguyen is a writer based in Charlotte, North Carolina.

NEW WORLD LIBRARY is dedicated to publishing books and other media that inspire and challenge us to improve the quality of our lives and the world.

We are a socially and environmentally aware company. We recognize that we have an ethical responsibility to our readers, our authors, our staff members, and our planet.

We serve our readers by creating the finest publications possible on personal growth, creativity, spirituality, wellness, and other areas of emerging importance. We serve our authors by working with them to produce and promote quality books that reach a wide audience. We serve New World Library employees with generous benefits, significant profit sharing, and constant encouragement to pursue their most expansive dreams.

Whenever possible, we print our books with soy-based ink on 100 percent postconsumer-waste recycled paper. We power our offices with solar energy and contribute to nonprofit organizations working to make the world a better place for us all.

Our products are available wherever books are sold. Visit our website to download our catalog, subscribe to our e-newsletter, read our blog, and link to authors' websites, videos, and podcasts.

customerservice@newworldlibrary.com
Phone: 415-884-2100 or 800-972-6657
Orders: Ext. 10 • Catalog requests: Ext. 10
Fax: 415-884-2199

www.newworldlibrary.com